LIFEBALANCE

Also by Linda and Richard Eyre
Published by Ballantine Books

Teaching Children Joy
Teaching Children Responsibility
Teaching Children Sensitivity

LIFEBALANCE

- Priority Balance
- Attitude Balance
- Goal Balance

In All Areas of Your Life

RICHARD and
LINDA EYRE

BALLANTINE BOOKS • NEW YORK

 Published in the United States by Ballantine Books, a division of Random House, Inc., New York, and simultaneously in Canada by Random House of Canada Limited, Toronto.

Library of Congress Cataloging-in-Publication Data

Eyre, Richard M.
Lifebalance.

1. Life skills—United States. 2. Time management—United States. I. Eyre, Linda. II. Title. III. Title: Life balance.
HQ2039.U6E97 1988 640′.43 86-48015
ISBN 0-345-34203-8

Design by Holly Johnson
Manufactured in the United States of America

First Edition: January 1988
10 9 8 7 6 5 4 3 2 1

CONTENTS

PROLOGUE

This book begins with some "lifescenes"—all too typical moments in all too typical lives. The reason some of them will seem so familiar is that you have already lived them. The reason we wrote this book is that *we* had already lived them . . . and wanted to stop.

This is a personal book. Almost every chapter has a couple of little boxed stories or incidents about our own family, our own discoveries and experiences, and our own frustrations and struggles to find lifebalance.

In a way, the book is a justification or a defense for the way we've chosen to live our lives—for our choice to put balance ahead of business and quality in front of quantity. It was a choice that took us a while to make, and that involved some interesting trade-offs, like fewer cocktail parties and more kite flying, fewer things and more time; trade-offs like giving up some major clients in order to spend a summer together as a family building a log cabin.

We view ourselves—and invite you to—not as experts or profound examples of *Lifebalance* but as a case study in the struggle. We're not speaking as those who have arrived and now shout back at you to follow. Rather, we've started a journey in a new direction toward a calmer, more balanced place. We invite you to travel with us.

Linda and Richard Eyre
Family-built log cabin
Blue Mountains—Eastern Oregon
September, 1987

P.S. We hope that as you read this becomes a personal book for you, too. One reason for the wide margins is to give you a space to make your own notes and observations about balance—so that when you finish the book, it will contain a lot of "your way" as well as a lot of ours.

LIFEBALANCE

LIFESCENES

Imagine a busy professional man, driving home from the airport after a week-long convention out of town. It's Saturday afternoon and he's anxious to see his family. The two or three weeks before the convention had been so hectic that he was getting home after dark every night and after the kids were in bed.

He turns onto his street and sees a small girl playing in his front yard. A friend of his daughter's, he guesses. She looks a little older than his daughter—maybe a new family has moved into the neighborhood. He wonders where Sammy is. She must be around, or this little friend wouldn't be here.

It is not until he pulls into the driveway and the girl runs toward the car that he realizes it *is* Samantha. How can she have grown that much? He feels a pang of joy as she reaches up to hug him—then a wave of guilt. His own daughter. For a minute he didn't recognize his own daughter.

Imagine a career woman, upwardly mobile, assertive, much of her identity wrapped up in her position in the firm, home now but still in her business suit. With her briefcase open on the kitchen table, appointment book in hand, she is trying to finish up some of the calls she didn't have time for at the office. She has been interrupted now several times by her four-year-old son, a round-faced little boy with big blue eyes.

"Mom . . . what's in that big book?"

"This is Mommy's appointment book, Timmy. What's in it are important things I have to do and the names of important people. Now, run upstairs and play with your toys."

Timmy wanders toward the stairway looking dejected. Then his face brightens and he turns back to his mom, tugs on her skirt. She looks down at him and says, through clenched teeth, "What *is* it, Timmy?"

"I just wondered, Mommy." Timmy's words are slow, his eyes pleading. "Is my name . . . in your book?"

Imagine the smell of old gym shoes. Tom is lacing them up for the first time in months. His doctor didn't mince words yesterday. "Tom, you've aged more than you should have since your last checkup. And your weight and your blood pressure are both going in the wrong direction." Things have been so hectic lately, Tom thinks;

there seems to be so little time, and so much stress. It's definitely time to get back into shape. It won't take that many workouts to get the old body on track again, he tells himself. I'm resilient; I can do it.

Tom has to sit down after a half mile at a slow trot. His knee hurts and his chest is burning. "What's happening to me?" he wonders. "What have I lost, and exactly where did I lose it?"

Imagine the pulse of the kettledrums and the throb of bass fiddles as the symphony begins. Kate shifts to the edge of her seat in anticipation. "It's been over a year since I've been to a concert," she thinks. Unbelievable. It used to be her life. No time anymore. The music lifts her, changes how her mind works, changes how the world looks.

"Who's the violinist in the third chair? It looks like . . . No, it couldn't be. She works, too—and has children, like I do." Kate squints and tries to see her facial features. "It is! She played behind me in the college orchestra. I haven't touched my violin for months—for years, really! How does she keep up? When does she practice?"

Kate doesn't feel happy for her old friend. She feels resentment. No, that isn't it. Yes . . . it is resentment. But not at the woman on the stage . . . at herself. She hasn't taken the time, hasn't found the time. And her talent is her love. And her talent is leaving her.

Imagine a wrinkled old family doctor, a general practitioner, just retired, reminiscing about his fifty years of broken bones, vaccinations, checkups, and especially about sitting at the bedsides of people about to die. "You know, it's interesting," he says. "You hear a lot of regrets from people on their deathbeds, but I'll tell you one I've never heard. No one ever says, 'If only I'd spent more time with the business.'"

Imagine the red sun setting behind the palms on a Caribbean island. The "M.B.A.," still in his tie from the afternoon convention session, has rolled up his trousers and is walking in the surf, hoping the sea breeze will clear his mind and help him sort out the production efficiency problems he has to face in three days when he returns to the office. He notices the windsurfer, the same fellow he met the day before, turning his board and setting out to catch one more wave.

"Poor guy," thinks the M.B.A. "How can he live without responsibility, without achievement? What will he ever have to show for his life?" In their conversation the day before, the windsurfer had told him that he did a little surfing instruction once in a while or rented out his board when he needed money, that he was leaving in a month to snow ski and work part-time in the Rockies.

The windsurfer notices the M.B.A. and waves. "What a jerk!" he thinks to himself. "Look at him in his suit pants and tie. Look at his gray hairs. I'll bet he's my age, but he looks ten years older. Wonder if he ever plans to *live*. He probably thinks he'll have some fun when he retires if he's not too fat or too old by then, or if he hasn't had a heart attack!"

Later that night the exhilaration and the day skips away a bit for both men. The M.B.A.'s mind keeps going back to the windsurfer, wondering whether production efficiency and a big salary really matter that much. The windsurfer keeps thinking about the M.B.A. and wonders if it's time to set some goals of his own to make a contribution of some kind. Maybe he should get a job this winter instead of skiing.

Imagine screaming! Two little, high-pitched voices trying to outyell each other. Is this a home or a torture chamber?

The housewife (she's got to think of another name for what she does—it's such a degrading title) yells back at her two children, hoping her ironic demand to "be quiet" will somehow prevail because of its superior decibel level.

When she is honest with herself, she realizes it's not her career she misses—well, she does miss work, too—but more than that, it's the *time* she had for herself. She misses getting ready in the morning, looking nice, getting complimented, and being alone once in a while.

Imagine paradise! That's what browsing in a bookstore feels like to Mary. I used to read, she thinks, I really did! And buy books. I knew what the latest ideas were—I got high on vicarious experiences and new theories. It takes energy to read, though. And I don't have any energy left after the job and the kids every day. I have to neglect something—I guess I've already chosen what it will be.

Imagine pressure. Two hours on this airplane and your secretary waiting at the airport to type the memo you're working on and get it out Federal Express, so New York will have it tomorrow morning.

And this person in the next seat wants to talk. A nice enough older lady, rather eccentric-looking. But why can't she see how busy you are? She's asked you three questions, and you've given three one-word answers. Finally she has taken the hint.

You finish the memo just in time, get off the plane, hand it to the waiting secretary. You notice the woman from the plane at the baggage claim and realize that she is probably a very interesting person. You find yourself vaguely wishing you had time to find out more about people—to talk to them to see how they view the world.

Imagine trying to explain this one to the Humane Society: The cat was bitten by the dog because the dog was in a bad temper because he had been kicked by Billy because Billy was upset because his mother yelled at him about leaving his coat on the chair because she was irritated because her husband had snapped at her because he felt uptight because his boss had criticized his monthly report because he felt a lot of stress because the president had called him on the carpet because he was worried because the board had raised the company's sales quota.

Imagine ripping a calendar to shreds—and enjoying it. It's too small anyway, too few hours in each day, too few days in each week. You sat down with your spouse to "coordinate schedules," but all you learned is that they wouldn't coordinate. Too many music lessons, too many late working hours, too many PTA meetings, too many Little League games, too many social commitments. You haven't even eaten together as a family for two or three weeks. You agree that you're "overcommitted," but you can't agree what to do about it.

Imagine a flat feeling. Scott and Anne are out together, celebrating their twentieth anniversary. The restaurant is beautiful, everything looks right, but their feelings are flat. There is less intensity in their love, less feeling when their hands touch, less fire—even in their disagreements. But they don't really love each other any less. Surely they don't. It's just that they're both so busy, right? A good, long talk will put everything right again—won't it?

Imagine being pulled in several different ways at once. That's how it feels coming home from work these days. Your wife needs something. Each of the children wants something. There are five dilemmas, three problems, and two conflicts that you are expected to solve. And the toilet ran over again. You thought there were pressures at work! Coming home is like jumping out of the frying pan and into the fire. Maybe working late would have been a good idea.

PART ONE

THE SYMPTOMS (OF UNBALANCE)

The "lifescenes" are the symptoms. And there are a lot more than the ones used to begin this book!

Busy people, doing so much, but somehow leaving out the most important things.

People who are tired enough to know they've been working hard yet still not too sure that anything worthwile is getting done.

People who get their jollies by crossing things off their "to do" list but who have lost their spontaneity.

People who live to work rather than working to live.

People who are always remembering how it was or thinking about how it will be.

People who read every article they see on stress and depression.

People who want to simplify, get back to the basics, and slow down but who never get around to doing so.

People who are reaching their goals but wondering if they are the right goals.

People who say they're happy but can't define happiness and wonder if they even understand the word.

People who are too busy "getting there" to enjoy the journey.

People who see their kids growing up too fast and their own lives going by too fast.

We all have our own symptoms.

And the diagnosis is unbalance.

LIFEBALANCE: THE PROBLEM OF OUR TIME—AND OF OUR PLACE

In the Western world before the industrial revolution the prevailing personal challenge was *survival.*

In the West following the industrial revolution the personal challenge was physical and economic *quality of life.*

In the West today the personal challenge is *balance.*

Because there are so many possibilities and responsibilities, it's hard to balance our *time.*

Because there are so many needs and demands, it's hard to balance our thought and our *attention.*

Because so many things are available, it's hard to balance our *resources* and desires.

And because we have so many options, alternatives, choices, and opportunities, it's hard to balance our *priorities.*

We have the same amount of mental energy and the same number of hours in a day as people of other generations and other locations, but we have so many more demands, so many more things.

We live in the first time and place in the world's history and geography where our challenges stem not from scarcity but from surplus, not from oppression but from options, and not from absence but from abundance.

Instead of struggling to find our next meal, we are struggling to get our busy families together long enough to eat a meal. Instead of fighting for freedom to make our choices, we are reeling in the complexity of eighty-three TV channels, tens of thousands of consumer items, and almost limitless numbers of education, job, and life-style alternatives.

It's not the sparse simplicity of too little but the crowded complexity of too much that plagues our lives. And the answers lie not in the balance of our abilities but in our ability to balance.

WHAT IS LIFEBALANCE AND ARE YOU SURE YOU WANT IT?

"Lifebalance," as you might have guessed, means the art of balancing such *finite* things as our time, our energy, and our thought among the seemingly *infinite* needs of our work, our families, and our personal interests and obligations.

Lifebalance also means the balance of our attitudes and approaches to life between the structured and the spontaneous, between fixed schedules and flexibility.

And finally, it implies balancing achievements with relationships, things with people, "getting" with "being."

Lifebalance involves doing something about our priorities and asking ourselves some hard questions about what is really important to us and about whether we are living our lives accordingly.

Balancing, for most of us, sounds like a pretty good idea (and like a very real need). But there is a warning that ought to come first, a factor you ought to consider before you adopt the goal of lifebalance—something you should ponder before you even decide to read this book.

It is simply this: People who live balanced lives can certainly succeed "in the world," but they may be less likely to have a bridge or a park or a fountain or a monument named after them. They may be less likely to become a solo artist with the Boston Philharmonic or to win the Nobel Prize for literature. And they are probably less likely to become U.S. senators or to form massive financial or business empires.

It is not impossible that balanced people will do these things, but they are less likely to do them than single-minded people who pursue them with all their time and all their energy. Diversified "Renaissance men" don't rule our world anymore. Specialists do.

If your goal is to get a bridge named after you, read a different book. But if you are occasionally touched by the vivid realization that this body and mind are the only ones you will ever develop, that this family is the only one you will ever raise, that this earth is the only one you will ever live on, that this life is the only one you will ever live (and that it is too short either to waste or to spend on one thing at the expense of everything else), then you are reading the right book, and we welcome you to the idea and the solution and the system of lifebalance.

And come to think of it, there is something of a backlash building up in our world against specialization and against directing all we have to narrow careers that force us into knowing more and more about less and less. It is a backlash against the whole idea of living to work instead of working to live . . . against the stress and competitiveness of our urban, materialistic society . . . and against the notion of forfeiting our bodies and our souls and our families for something that the world mistakenly calls success.

So who knows; the world may be changing, and it may once again name its bridges after balanced men and balanced women.

And our children and our associates, if they don't put our names on monuments, may put our examples into their lives, and our memories into their hearts.

LOCATING THE EPIDEMIC (IT'S ALL AROUND US)

When unbalance occurs in a circus, it is very easy to see. The man on the high wire slips, loses his confidence, begins to wobble, and in the audience our hearts jump into our throats. Or the juggler loses his concentration, drops one ball, and haplessly tries to catch the others as they fall out of orbit. We look away, embarrassed for him.

In life, unbalance is a little harder to see. People become rather good at hiding the stress and frustration they feel. They conceal the worry that things aren't right in their families and the fact that they are neglecting crucial things like their own bodies, their own minds, and their own children in favor of less crucial things like social ladders and career ladders.

But we don't hide our unbalance from ourselves. Thoreau said we live "lives of quiet desperation." Whatever we call it, we know our lives are at least a little out of balance. Some of us are so painfully aware of our unbalance that we think Thoreau's description was an understatement. Others of us are just occasionally pierced by a needle of unbalance as we long for a little more solitude, or time to think, or time to relax with our families, or simply for a slower, more flexible, more meaningful lifestyle. And sometimes, in the pure joy of a spontaneous moment or an unexpected brand-new friendship, we stop and wonder why it doesn't happen to us more often. We feel creative urges, emotional tugs, adventuresome parts of us stirring within, but there's no time for them—there isn't even time for the things we have to do.

We talk quite a bit these days about stress, about emptiness, about unbalance. But our talk is usually just commiseration—about how bad it is, how impossible it is to do anything about it, and that at least we're not alone; everyone feels it. . . .

Once in a while, though, we're encouraged (or maybe discouraged) by someone who seems to be covering all the bases, keeping the balls in the air, and walking the tightrope with apparent ease—even with pleasure. And he doesn't seem stressed either. He hasn't lost his sense of fun or spontaneity, and he's not even rushed or hassled. How come? Does he have more hours in his day than we do in ours? Does he need less sleep? Is the world and what's important in it somehow clearer and simpler to him? Is he simply more talented?

None of the above! Unbalance may *seem* to be a product of the world around us, but we actually cause it for ourselves—by the way we live, the way we plan, the way we think.

This book is nothing less than an attempt to help you change the way you plan, and thus the way you think, and thus the way you function and balance your life. It will not give you some magic formula for how to do everything at once, but it will suggest some ways to decide what's important and what isn't—and it will suggest a system of planning and of thinking that will keep the important things (and the important parts of ourselves) in balance.

If you simply want to increase the *quantity* of things you get done in a day, almost any planning, scheduling, or time management program will help.

But if you are more interested in improving the *quality* of the things you do each day, then *Lifebalance* was written for you. Rather than attempting to help you get more done, it will encourage you to do fewer unimportant things in order to do more about the important things in your life.

But wait; before we talk about the cures or about the preventive medicine that can keep us balanced and well, let's be sure we recognize the sickness and self-diagnose the specific areas in which we each have difficulty with balance. The short "tests" that follow are designed to help us recognize and define our own particular unbalance.

TWO SHORT "BALANCE TESTS"

It's common in our world, when you don't feel quite right, to "take a few tests." If you wonder just *where* your life is out of balance, the following tests may help you to find out. But be careful; they may prove there is more unbalance in your life than you had thought. (Or they may confirm some things you really already knew but hadn't fully admitted to yourself.)

Be candid and honest on the questions. These are private tests, and if anyone *corrects* them, it will be you! And don't let the results worry you. Remember, unbalance is the norm in our world, and it can't be corrected until it is discovered.

TEST 1.

On a blank sheet of paper or on the spaces printed here, prioritize the four following things. Write them in the space below, in order of how much they mean to you, with the most important element listed first.

Work or Career	Personal Character (including beliefs, inner growth, etc.)	Family	Other Interests (including recreation, TV, etc.)

1. ____________________
2. ____________________
3. ____________________
4. ____________________

When you have finished, turn the paper over (or use the margin of this page) and list the same four things again, only this time put them in order of how much time and thought you spend on each.

TEST 2.

Go through the following questions in sequence, jotting brief answers in the lines provided or on a separate, numbered sheet of paper. If a question seems hard, or obscure, or takes too much thought, skip it and go on to the next question. Don't go back to the questions you skipped until you read the paragraphs following the test.

1. What was the most recent advancement, promotion, or raise you received at work? ________________

____

____

____

2. Do you have any written goals for your marriage? (If so, what are they?) ________________

____

____

____

3. Think quickly of a thing you are better at or a way in which you are better off than the neighbors living on each side of you. ________________

____

____

____

4. Name the latest discovery you have made about the nature or potential or talent of someone in your immediate family. ________________

____

____

____

5. What are two "achievement goals" you have for this year (two things you would like to accomplish)?

____

____

____

6. Recall the last important discovery you made about yourself. ______________________________

____

____

____

7. What specific five-year goals do you have financially or for your career? ______________________

____

____

____

8. What is your latest personal, creative effort? (When did you last write a poem, paint, etc.?) ______________

____

____

____

9. What are your best skills and abilities at work? What attributes contribute to your success? __________

____

____

____

10. What are your best skills and most natural abilities as a spouse and as a parent? __________________

____

____

____

11. What is the last thing you've read relating to your career or field of work? _____________________

____

____

____

12. What are the last two books you've read for relaxation or out of an interest unrelated to your career?

____

13. Name the three biggest challenges you currently face at work.

14. What are the three most important things you want to give to your children?

15. Whom do you admire most for accomplishments?

16. Whom do you admire most for sensitivity?

17. Name the last project you carefully planned and executed.

18. What is the last completely spontaneous thing you can remember doing?

19. Think back over last week. What is the most important thing you accomplished? ______________________

____

____

____

20. Think again over the past week. What is the most playful or silly thing you did? ______________________

____

____

____

21. What is your favorite time management or planning system? ______________________________

____

____

____

22. When did you last participate in an exciting discussion of ideas unrelated to your work? ____________

____

____

____

23. What is the last thing you got really excited about doing? ______________________________________

____

____

____

24. When was the last time you felt completely relaxed? ______________________________________

____

____

____

25. When did you last apply "positive mental attitude" to a situation? ______________________________

26. How many good belly laughs have you enjoyed this week?

27. Did you make some lists of things to do this last week and cross them off as you did them?

28. What is the most beautiful aspect of nature you noticed last week?

29. Name the last problem you figured out, analyzed, and solved.

30. When did you last have a "flash insight" or an answer or insight that just seemed to come out of nowhere? What was it?

31. List three or four things that you discipline yourself to do every day.

32. What was the best question you thought of or pondered this week?

33. What is the most exciting thing you've purchased lately (your newest possession or "toy")?

34. When is the last time you had a personal spiritual experience or felt deeply moved by something?

35. What is one thing you'd really like to buy right now if you had enough money?

36. Name two people you plan to get to know better simply because they seem like interesting people.

37. What are the things in your wardrobe that you absolutely could not get along without?

38. Name two people who have confided in you lately.

39. Name one or two of the best new business contacts you have made recently.

40. Think of a good friend. What are his or her two biggest needs?

41. Of whom do you feel just a little bit jealous?

42. Who is the most interesting stranger you have had a conversation with lately?

Let's talk about the second test first—the one you just finished. We'll go back to the first test in a moment. On the second (forty-two-question) test, there are no "right" or "wrong" answers. The real "test" has to do with which questions were easier for you to answer. A quick tip-of-the-tongue answer indicates that you are *oriented* to the subject of that question—or at least that you think a lot about it.

If you look back over the test, you will realize that the odd-numbered questions have to do with work and career, with structured thinking, and with achievements. The even-numbered questions deal more with family and personal growth, with spontaneity and with relationships.

On the first sixteen questions, if the odd numbers were easiest, you are more occupied with work and career than with family and personal growth. If the "evens" were easy and the "odds" hard, you may be too family- and character-development-oriented. (You are also a distinct minority.)

On the second sixteen questions (through number thirty-two), easier odds point to an unbalance of too much structure and too little spontaneity (and vice versa).

On the last ten questions, easier odds suggest you are too achievement-oriented. Easier evens (a rarity) indicate that you may be so conscious of other people that you don't accomplish much yourself.

Now let's go back to the first test. As we have used it in seminars around the country, a consistent (and somewhat disturbing) pattern has become clear. Most people list their priorities (on the front side) in the following order:

1. Family
2. Personal character (including beliefs, education, inner growth, etc.)
3. Work or career
4. Other interests (including recreation, TV, etc.)

Sometimes numbers 1 and 2 are reversed, and sometimes 3 switches with 4. But the majority list them as they appear above.

On the "other side," when listed in order of time and thought spent, the list is often *reversed*.

1. Other interests (including recreation, TV, etc.)
2. Work or career
3. Personal character (including beliefs, education, inner growth, etc.)
4. Family

Careful calculation (of time and thought expended) sometimes puts "other interest" (often over forty hours a week) above work and career. With many people, work or career is first, but the two are almost always well ahead of personal and family.

Some might say that the test is unfair—that we *have* to spend forty or more hours a week working and simply don't have the luxury of putting more important things first. But even when the *time* measurement is removed and we rank things in order of the *thought* we give them, the priority list is still basically reversed.

So . . . whatever the reasons are, and wherever the blame rests, the point is that our list of priorities and our list of how we spend our time and our thought are opposites. We know what is most important, but that knowledge does not translate into how we live our lives. And therein lies the well-justified concern that most of us feel about unbalance.

PART TWO

THE SITUATION (WHO OR WHAT IS TO BLAME?)

What causes unbalance? When stress and frustration (or exhaustion) remind us that we are out of balance, whom do we blame?

When the tightrope walker slips or the juggler's tenpins bounce off each other and clatter to the floor . . . it's nice if there is something to *blame.* Maybe the tightrope was loose, or a tenpin was slippery; perhaps flashbulbs distracted; maybe there was even a slight earth tremor.

And our own unbalanced lives need an external explanation, too, don't they? After all, our parents and grandparents didn't feel the stress that we do, so it must be something in our world—something now in our world.

Now, theoretically we ought to be the most relaxed people on earth and in history. Our technology frees most of us from backbreaking work and from the necessary manual labor that dominated the worlds of our forebearers. When we read their journals and diaries or listen to their reminiscing, we hear of eras with less stress, less scrambling, and somehow with more time and maybe more meaning.

So let's find the culprit! Let's find whom or what we can blame and get on with it.

TODAY'S WORLD?

No world has ever bombarded its occupants with more options, saturated them with more stress, or pitted them against each other in more relentless competition.

Is it the best of times or the worst of times? Our technological advances and our information revolution have multiplied what we can know, what we can do, where we can go. The options are endless. One person subscribes to twenty-two magazines, another gets eighty-three TV channels, another claims to have visited more than forty countries on discounted airfares, still another has taken up a different new sport every year for fifteen years.

Rags-to-riches stories abound. Anyone can "make it" in America, and more do—every day. The competition is fierce, but there are so many competitors and so many who seem to be winning. Instead of working to live, many of us live to work. Our identity is largely our job. The first question we ask people is "What do you do?"

Our world has been described as one in which people

worship their work,
work at their play,
and play at their worship.

Too often we measure (and are measured) by position, title, income, appearance, credentials, contacts. It's easy to forget (or never even look for) things like character, beliefs, integrity, commitment.

It has been said that what is wrong with us, and wrong with the world we live in, can be summarized in two words:

Too much

There is too much materialism, too much advertising, too much leisure, too much entertainment, too much passive time wasting (e.g., TV), too many books with too many self-improvement ideas, too many vacation options, too many new car models, too much complexity, too much access to information, too much hustling, too many traffic jams, too many people, too many talk shows! The list itself is too much.

At times we long for the good old days—or for some good old place where we grew up, or where our folks grew up—a simpler place, a simpler time. But then we remember the things they *didn't* have then. And we remember the things they *did* have then, like confinement and poverty and basic illnesses without basic cures—and we realize in many ways that those were the "bad old days."

We also realize, when we stop and think, that today,

despite its stress and complexity, is not the worst of times for balance. At least we're talking about it. The idea of balanced lives is in vogue. We're looking for balance and realizing that financial and career success is *not* all there is. The self-gratification of the 1970s is being replaced by greater interest in commitment and parenting. The "me generation" is being replaced by the "we generation." Committed feminists are having babies and staying home with them. Business conventions hear speakers on "quality of life" instead of salesmanship, positive mental attitude, or winning through intimidation.

So . . . do we blame unbalance on the world . . . on the times? Certainly there is a lot "out there" that contributes to unbalance—but can we blame the world for our personal unbalance? Not really. Not quite.

Let's try some other suspects.

BIGNESS AND MATERIALISM?

We're surrounded by institutions that control our lives and by "messages" that make counterfeit connections between materialism and happiness.

We're just little organisms—five or six feet of entity—functioning in a land of inorganic giants: giant corporations, giant government, giant bureaucracies, giant schools of thought. They tell us what to do, what not to do, when, how. The giants fill our lives with busywork, forms, meetings, and memos. We are their subjects or their moving parts or the markers on their game boards—moved here and there, squeezed, taxed, categorized, used.

And if that's not enough, there are voices out there in the giants' throats. So *many* voices, telling us what we should want, what we should seek, what we should do. Twelve hundred advertising messages are received each week through the sensory apparatus of a single human pawn—moving us, pulling us, blurring the lines between wants and needs, and linking those carefully cultivated covetings into a kind of counterfeit contentment based on a promised happiness that doesn't happen.

"It is the preoccupation with possession, more than anything else, that prevents men from living freely and nobly." Bertrand Russell said it, but few are listening. The giants and their voices are too big and too loud, and how can we balance lives that we don't control? Some of us idly wonder if maybe the institutions will balance us . . . by giving us flextime and on-site nurseries so we can be with our children, or by giving us solitude rooms so we can be with ourselves, or by building environments conducive to relationships or spontaneity. And maybe the "voices" will balance us with self-help ideas or public-service spots on the joys of families.

Don't hold your breath. The giants are interested in themselves, not in us. They are interested in the products, not the people. We're their customers, or their slaves, or cogs in their machines. Since when did a master worry if his valet was living a balanced life—so long as he was good at shining shoes?

No—it's ridiculous to think big institutions and big advertising will correct our individual unbalance. . . . But it is also ridiculous to believe that they *caused* it.

Because we *do* choose. Big as the "giants" are, they cannot control us unless we let them. We choose whom we work for, what we want, whom we envy, where we'll be led.

So let's keep looking for the culprit in the still-unsolved crime of unbalance.

SPECIALIZATION AND "COVETING COMPETITIVENESS"?

Thomas Jefferson was once described as "a man of thirty-two who can try a case, design an edifice, fight a duel, break a horse, write a treatise, dance a minuet, invent the swivel chair, and play the violin."

A few hundred years before him Leonardo da Vinci, also an expert horseman and fencer, discovered and thoroughly understood human and animal anatomy and also managed to create a glider and a parachute; develop jacks, winches, lathes, pulleys, springs, and roller bearings; and invent the crane, the piston, the differential transmission, and air-inflated skis for walking on water. He also, by the way, painted the *Mona Lisa* and the *Last Supper*.

For a period starting around the time of da Vinci and

ending not long after Jefferson, the idea of the Renaissance man won the world's admiration and aspiration.

Then came the industrial age, and with it specialization. Instead of being small, versatile, self-contained, and self-sufficient machines, people began to be little, interdependent parts of big machines.

And the individual "machine parts," or segmented little fields of knowledge or expertise, became so *deep* that people began to have to spend all their time just getting to the bottom of them.

With industrialization came urbanization. People began living closer to each other and comparing themselves in more ways with more other people. Mass media and advertising came along to help our wants outpace our needs. Picking out one little thing and trying to know more about it and do better at it than anyone else became the most predictable path to the newly revalued prizes of prominence and prosperity.

The single-mindedness required was bad for balance. More thought, time, and effort went into work, less into family and personal growth; more importance was placed on structure, less on spontaneity; more attention went to achievements, less to relationships.

Today we have moved from the industrial age to the information age. Our machines are more sophisticated, and our access to information and technology is dramatically increased. Theoretically, we have more leisure time, more freedom, more wealth and convenience, and therefore more opportunity to broaden ourselves, to take time for all of our priorities, and to balance our lives. But specialization keeps getting narrower, competitiveness and materialism keep getting sharper, and we have to be work-oriented, highly structured, and "in the fast lane" just to keep up!

Gone are the Renaissance men who cultivated varied interests and ideas, tried many things, and lived fully alive lives. Here are the tight-lipped, one-dimensional, one-directional people whose lives seem somehow shortened by their narrowness.

If we keep getting more specialized, the theory goes, we will continue to learn more and more about less and less until we will ultimately know everything about nothing.

Many of us feel that we have been forced to give up the idea of being "well rounded" in favor of the goal of being "highly sharpened."

To "make it" in a given career seems to require (1) endless study of a specialized field, (2) long apprenticeships gaining experience in some still-smaller subset of that field, and (3) staying constantly updated and on top of further dimensions and new, specialized knowledge within the field.

It's tough enough to be a good high-speed microprocessor designer or a good diversified production company tax accountant, but to be that *and* a good father, a good husband, a good catamaran sailor, a good musician, good amateur film critic, and a good school board member—*that* is a real trick.

You can try to be all of these, but watch out, because the guy who was only trying for the first one will get the next promotion and, balanced or not, you'll end up working for him.

So . . . we can blame our stress and unbalance on specialization and competiveness . . . right?

Wrong! We can perhaps blame the *world's* unbalance on these things. But our own unbalance is too personal to blame on something as impersonal as specialization. We have lives and identities that are separate and apart, that belong to us. We do not have to be defined by what is happening in the world around us.

So let's look deeper.

UNREALISTIC EXPECTATIONS AND RESPONSIBILITIES?

Everyone seems to need more and expect more than we can give. Our parents, our teachers, our boss, our children, our spouse, our club, our political party, the church, the PTA . . . and ourselves. All of these "demanders" have got us where they want us. They have us "reporting to them," and they can call us anytime on the phone (and usually do).

Even the government apparently needs us—it must, because it taxes us, and has us report in all kinds of ways. Not only big, wasteful bureaucracies, but big, misguided causes shove us around and wrap our minds with notions that increase our pressures and decrease our freedom. Misguided liberalism tries to make the government the solution for all problems and succeeds only in building bureaucracies and raising the tide of taxes. Misguided conservatism tries to turn back the clock and make us feel guilty about some of the advances we have made. Misguided sexism tries to deny women the workplace and demands that women always be at home, even after their children are in school. Misguided feminism tells women they should have it all—and have it all at once—career and children, family and future, marriage and more of everything, thus pressuring away the logical approach of dividing life into seasons and focusing certain periods on certain opportunities and priorities that won't ever come back for a second chance.

Books and media keep holding up images of super-moms and do-it-all macho-men that make us feel guilty and inadequate.

And then there are the demands we put on ourselves. Some of them come from well-intended clichés and other bits of "common wisdom" that only add to the pressure.

"Get involved."

"If something is worth doing, it's worth doing well."

"Never turn down worthwhile church or civic assignments."

"Haste makes waste."

"Give your children everything—give them your time."

"Always do what is asked, and then do a little more."

"Ask what you can do for your country."

"There is always room at the top."

So many needs, so many expectations from others and from ourselves. Even extra hours in the day wouldn't help that much because lots of the demands come at the same time.

If we could clone ourselves, if there were two of us . . . or three, maybe we could satisfy everyone.

Do all of these demands make us unbalanced?

Or do they just demand balance?

AMBITION AND "OVERSTRUCTURED" LIVES?

It might seem reasonable to assume that a rather good antidote for unbalance would be planning, scheduling, list making, and organizing.

On the contrary! The way most people plan, and the planning tools they use, actually aggravate their unbalance more than they alleviate it.

For example, let's consider a fairly typical businessman who uses a fairly typical schedule book or timer organizer. If we take his planning book and analyze its contents, we will find three things: First we find that more than 95 percent of his entries (lists, plans, appointments, reminders, etc.) have to do with his work. It's hard to find anything relating to his family or to his own personal growth. Second, his "planning" leaves no time for spontaneity or flexibility. He prides himself on "using every hour of the day," and he gets his kicks from checking off everything on "his list." His motto is "act, don't react," and he likes to say that people who are good planners hate surprises and avoid them by only allowing things to happen if they are on their list. Third, just as there's no room on his schedules for spontaneity and surprises, there's precious little space for relationships. Planning and lists seem to deal much more with things than with people.

Perhaps it's unfair to say that typical list making, planning, and scheduling *causes* unbalance, but it does often *compound* the problem and *contribute* to a lack of balance between work, family, and self, between structure and spontaneity, and between relationship and achievements.

All our dreaming and scheming, all our objectives and plans may "get us ahead," but they may also aggravate and compound our unbalance.

OURSELVES?

It's easy to blame unbalance on our world or our institutions or our responsibilities, but it doesn't do any good. All we can balance is ourselves.

Samuel Johnson put it very succinctly: "He who has so little knowledge of human nature as to seek happiness by changing anything but his own disposition will waste his life in fruitless efforts and multiply the grief he proposes to remove."

There are two important things to realize here. One is that it doesn't do any good to blame unbalances on the people or the things or the situations and circumstances around us. Two is the hopeful and optimistic realization that whatever the outside forces are, we have the capacity to balance ourselves, to set our own priorities, and to follow the drummer we hear. Our influence over ourselves can be far stronger than any other influence.

We once heard a man tell of observing an iceberg in the Arctic ocean. A gale-force wind was blowing, causing the snow and ice particles on the iceberg to stream horizontally in one direction. Yet the iceberg was moving steadily and somewhat rapidly *in the opposite direction*. The reason was the current. The current was less visible than the wind, but far more powerful.

The currents in our lives are generated by our choices. The world with its materialism, competitiveness, and busyness may swirl around us, blowing us toward unbalance and stress, but the currents created by our choices and the habits we choose to develop can propel us in opposite directions, toward the quality of life found in meaningful, prioritized living.

The world may drive us into unbalance, but we can drive ourselves out!

Let's think about it through an additional metaphor:

There once was a preschool which had one unit in its curriculum on "goal setting." A three-and-a-half-year-old boy, after hearing some stories that explained the idea of goals to him, decided his goal would be to stop sucking his thumb.

The preschool teacher was concerned because she wanted all the children to reach their goals, and this child, who reminded her of Linus in the Peanuts comic strip, had a severe thumb-sucking problem, which also involved dragging around a tattered old blanket which he rubbed with the thumb and forefinger of one hand while sucking the thumb of the other hand.

"'Linus' was insistent, however—that *was* his goal."

The teacher didn't realize just how intent the little boy was until a couple of days later when he came to her and said, "Teacher, I just don't think I'm going to be able to give up my thumb as long as I have the blanket. Here, will you put it up on the refrigerator, where I can't feel it?"

Unbalance in our lives results from bad habits—habits that emphasize work at the expense of family and personal growth, or structure at the expense of spontaneity, or accomplishments at the expense of relationships (or vice versa on any of the above).

These bad habits may have to do with the way we think, or the way we plan or don't plan, or simply with the way we live our lives each day.

To blame our habits of unbalance on the world, or on the materialism around us, or on the responsibilities and demands on our time would be a lot like blaming the habit of thumb sucking on the blanket.

The blanket may be *contributing* to the problem, and removing the blanket's influence from our lives may help us to change, but the problem is the habit, and we change our habits only by changing ourselves.

Let's look more closely at some of the bad habits which we develop and which tend to unbalance our lives—and at some of the "Linus blankets" which make them hard habits to break.

1. Partly because of the "blanket" of peer pressure and competitive specialization, many of us get in the habit of using all our time and mental energy on our work and having none left over for family and personal needs.

2. Partly because of the "blanket" of too many responsibilities and the complexity and busyness of our

lives, we often get in the habit of too many lists and so much structure that there is no room for spontaneity or surprises, for flexibility or fun.

3. Partly because of the "blanket" of the fast pace of our world and its rampant materialism, most of us get in the habit of not communicating very well about our feelings and of measuring ourselves much more on the quantity of our achievements than on the quality of our relationships.

This is a book about putting our "blankets up on the refrigerator," where we can't feel them—but more than that, it is a book about changing our habits.

The next section, called "The Solution," is about getting rid of old blankets and old habits and developing some new and more balanced ways of thinking and of looking at life.

The last section, called "The Summary," is about developing some new habits that will keep the old ones from coming back—and keep the blankets up on the refrigerator.

INTERMISSION: REVIEWING WHERE WE ARE BEFORE WE LOOK FOR A WAY OUT

This book has an intermission for the same reason that concerts and plays do—to give you a chance to stretch, to wander around a bit, to reflect and evaluate, or discuss what's happened so far, and to anticipate what's to come and wonder how it will all end.

It also gives us a chance to point out that Act II (what follows) is a *cure* but not a *chore.* Lifebalance, as we will present it, is an antidote for unbalance, but it is not bitter medicine. It is, in fact, rather tasty. It is also an exciting challenge. What we are dealing with here is the art of living life!

Yes, our lives are complex—but that is just another way of saying that they are interesting. It is a demanding, competitive world, but few of us would trade it for "the bad old days."

The suggestions that follow constitute something that is more an art than a science. Most self-help, how-to, time-and-self management books are written like a science, where we are told what to do like robots being programmed. A science separates and categorizes things—while art seeks to combine and merge things in a creative and enjoyable way. We'd like you to view what follows as the *art* of lifebalance.

Some of the suggestions in the next section are things that you personally may not need. Read them for interest if you like, but don't bother with them. You'll recognize the ones you need. Focus on these—*fasten onto them and use them.*

After you've picked out the particular suggestions you need (and like), we'll show you an all-new planning system (some call it antiplanning because it's so different from traditional time management) that will help you to implement the kinds of balance you need.

And don't hesitate to alter the ideas that appeal to you. Change them where you like to make them fit you better. If you read a suggestion, and like it, but feel there is a better way to apply it—or if you *don't* like a solution but it makes you think of one you *do* like—then write it into the book's wide margin. Rewrite the book wherever you like to make it *your* book—*your* lifebalance. After all, it's your book now; you bought it. And, more important, it's your life—your life to balance.

And consider one other thing before the intermission is over. Our grandparents in this country did not face the challenge of lifebalance. Their minds were occupied with other concerns—like *survival.*

It is the bounty of our world, the wideness of our horizons, the diversity and options of our lives that make lifebalance our concern. It is the topic and challenge of our times. We should relish it and be grateful for it. Lifebalance is an art which can allow us to say, with Suzuki, "I'm an artist at living, and my art is my life."

PART THREE

THE SOLUTION: (THREE KINDS OF BALANCE)

After discussing the wideranging symptoms of a problem as difficult and complete as unbalance, we're aware that a section title like "The Solution" may sound a little presumptuous. . . . So let us define and defend the term.

Just as the symptoms of unbalance vary from person to person, so must the prescriptions be individual. And only self-diagnosis and self-prescription will work. There is no cure-all medicine, and there is no one person who can diagnose or cure everyone (or anyone) else.

Therefore, by "solution" we mean your solution, not ours. The thirty short chapters that follow (nine or ten each plus a summary on priority balance, on attitude balance, and on goal balance) are *ideas*. . . . They are possibilities—and you can try the ones that you relate to or feel a need for. Out of them, and out of your own ideas, we hope you will formulate a "balance combination" that works for you.

All writers make assumptions about their readers. Ours about you are straightforward. We assume you are concerned about balance (or we deduce it from the fact that you bought the book). But we also assume you have strong ideas of your own about your priorities, about your needs, about how you want to live your life.

So we don't expect you to implement or even to agree with everything we say. In fact, it would worry us if you did.

We invite you to use what you like from this section and to view what we say not as instruction but as stimulation.

Think of this section as a springboard. If, as you read, you begin to feel that there is too much on the table, remind yourself that you don't have to eat it all. A wide variety of balanced meals can be made with different combinations from the same menu, particularly when you bring along a few favorite recipes of your own.

Each short chapter is essentially a principle of balance followed by specific and direct suggestions on how to implement it. You will relate to some of them the minute you read them. Others you will feel that you have already mastered or that you simply don't need. Still others will fall somewhere in between—you will not know right away just how relevant or how workable they would be for you. Try them out for a short time, and depending on how they "feel," either continue them or discard them.

Now let's begin by deciding just what it is that we're trying to balance.

Our first impression might be that it is our *time* that must be balanced. We schedule it, we juggle it, we stretch it, and mostly we just wish there were more of it. But there will never be enough time to balance until we balance *ourselves*—until we balance our priorities and our plans, our attitudes and our attention, our goals and our gifts.

There are three separate kinds of unbalance that plague our lives: three kinds of balancing we need to become adept at if we want to improve the quality of our lives.

The first we will call *priority balance*—the balance between family, career, and personal needs. It involves an increased awareness of what is important and an ability to balance our thought and our effort among the things that really matter. It requires a new way of planning. Not the typical scheduling where we sit down and think "Now . . . what do I have to do?" Instead, *Lifebalance* will suggest a new kind of balanced planning where we ask ourselves questions like "What do I *choose* to do?" or "What *should* I do?" or even "What do I *want* to do?"

The second we will call *attitude balance*—the balance between structure and spontaneity. It involves the skill of being both firm and flexible, both disciplined and dreamy. It involves being aware and watching for unanticipated needs and unplanned opportunities, and it requires some serendipity to go along with our schedules. Lifebalance will propose a form of balanced planning that provides for and enhances the *unplanned*.

The third we will call *goal balance*—the balance between achievements and relationships, between people and things. Lifebalance involves setting aside some time for communicating, for listening, for understanding, and it introduces a new kind of objective called "relationship goals," which are quite different from the achievement goals we are more accustomed to.

Let's revert one last time to our circus analogy. Imagine a three-ring circus. In one ring is the juggler, keeping all his balls in the air. In the second ring is the tightrope walker, and in the third a teeter-totter where the acrobats on one side balance those on the other.

Three kinds of balance. Now imagine the three rings of lifebalance. Priority balance in the first ring. It's a matter of selecting which balls are important and then gaining the skills to keep them all in the air at once. Attitude balance in the second ring is a matter of staying upright on life's rope by not slipping too far toward the structure or too far to the spontaneity side. And goal balance in the third ring requires enough weight on the relationship side of the teeter-totter to counterweigh the efforts we make on achievement.

This section of *Lifebalance* will make a series of observations and suggestions about each of the three types of balance, and will present nine or ten principles for each of the three.

Select the ones you like and need.

A. PRIORITY BALANCE (BALANCING WORK WITH FAMILY WITH SELF)

The first type of balance is *priority balance.*

Conceptually, it is simple, even obvious. We should know what is important to us . . . and we should spend our time and our thought on the high priorities rather than the low ones.

But in reality, in the day-to-day, it is not so simple. There is little correlation between how important things are to us and how much thought or effort we give to them. We constantly find ourselves wishing we had time for the really important things, wishing there were more hours in the day, wishing life were less complex, and wishing we were better at juggling all the things we need to do.

The principles of this priority balance section are intended to help us stop wishing and start changing.

1. SIMPLIFYING AND PERSPECTIVE

"Why should we be in such desperate haste?" said Thoreau, "And in such desperate enterprises?" And why do we let ourselves want so much and get so busy and burdened?

When will we learn that the trade we so often make of time and freedom for things and excess involvement is a bad deal? And when will our society outgrow the rather juvenile notion that big and complex is better than small and simple?

"Besides the noble art of getting things done," said an Oriental philosopher named Lin Yu Tang, "there is the more noble art of leaving things undone." We admire the Gandhis of the world, who get rid of everything but their eyeglasses, Scripture and loincloth so they can focus on what is important. But we don't emulate them.

The ability to see things in clear perspective and the art of simplifying can be gradually learned by developing the habit of asking ourselves four questions:

- Will it matter in ten years?
- What do I need more of in my life?
- What do I need less of?
- How can I make this simpler?

With the habit of these questions will come some new skills—the skill of "discretionary neglect," the skill of saying no, the skill of deciding what *not* to do, the skill of discerning which things are worth doing well . . . and which things are just worth doing . . . and which things are not worth doing at all.

Linda:

Dropping off the car pool one day, I stopped to visit with a busy mother who was in the process of designing an elaborate three-layer cake. "It's for the church anniversary party," she explained, "and I thought I'd better make it really special." She mentioned that she thought the "dramatic" cake she had in mind would take her fifteen to twenty hours. I knew she had several children, a part-time job, and a whole lot of other demands on her time, so I asked her why? Did she enjoy making elaborate cakes? Had someone told her it had to be that big or that special? Was she trying to teach something to her children? Was she doing penance?

No—none of these. The only reason she could think of for the extensive project was that she'd always believed "if something is worth doing, it's worth doing well."

Not really—not always! Some things, in relation to the real priorities, are just barely worth doing at all and ought to be simplified down to "quick and easy" rather than blown up to "elaborate and time-consuming." We decided a better saying would be "If a thing is just barely worth doing, then just barely do it!"

She decided (with relief) to make a nice, innocuous cake from an easy recipe that took one hour.

"Adding on" too often complicates our lives and contributes to the loss of self. "Casting off" simplifies our lives and helps us find ourselves.

Get in the habit of asking the four questions!

Get rid of what you don't need!

Acquire a few very fine things! (One nice piece in an otherwise empty place is more attractive than a room full of rubbish.)

Reduce your wants! Understand that there are two definitions of financial independence. One is having enough money to buy everything you want; the other is wanting less than what you are able to buy.

Simplify!

Simplify!

2. THINGS THAT MATTER

Linda

We took all eight children to Mexico one summer and spent six weeks in Ajijic, a little mountaintop fishing village near Guadalajara. Richard was writing a novel and needed background material and solitude, but the primary reason for our trip was to give the children perspective.

Because we had no car while we were there, we arranged for horseback transportation. A little Mexican man would arrive every third day with eight horses (the smallest two children rode double) and peso signs gleaming in his eyes at such a large account. (It cost approximately twelve dollars to rent eight horses for one hour.)

As our caravan meandered along the beach, we saw the village women pounding their washing on the rocks, and when we clip-clipped through the village streets, we saw families with ten children in one room. With eyes wide, our children gazed into the eyes of the native children, whose eyes also showed amazement. (I don't know who was seeing the better show.)

One little nine-year-old girl visited our Mexican-style condominium every day. Too shy to venture in at first, she became braver each day as she watched the children play in the small front-yard swimming pool. Neatly dressed in the same blue dress and no shoes, she was always smiling and happy and came day after day to interact with the children (who were not the least bit bothered with the language barrier), but turned down all our invitations to go swimming with us. On the last Wednesday before we left, she finally consented to swim. We were all amazed when she came at the appropriate time and jumped in the pool in her blue dress. At that moment we realized that she had no swimming suit or shoes—nothing besides the dress that she wore.

Our leftover food went to her family on the day that we left. When we delivered it, we found a happy family in a home with only three walls and a muddy front yard, complete with a cow, a pig, and two chickens.

Many valuable lessons were learned that summer, not the least of which was that one does not need brand-name clothes or even shoes, to be happy!

Unlike the problems of the people in Ajijic, Mexico, the problems of "fast-track" Americans do not stem from scarcity or lack of options of challenges. Instead, our test is whether we can sort out and choose the most important and meaningful things from among all the needs and demands and options that surround us.

The most important things in life need to be elevated above the countless other things that compete for our time and attention. Before we worry about the methods and techniques of balance, we need to decide and categorize which things are worth balancing.

We asked a group of people what needs or aspects of their lives they were trying to get in balance. It was like opening a dam or triggering an avalanche. We were trying to make a list on a blackboard, but it was hard to write fast enough.

career
children
spouse
recreation

sleep
church obligations
PTA
social engagements
hobbies
reading for recreation
exercise—fitness
travel
lessons (piano, dancing, etc.)
reading to stay informed
civic involvement
clubs
talents (using them, developing them)
television
kids' soccer
solitude
care of car and other possessions
appearance (care of self)
culture, music
Little League
social and friends
relatives (staying in touch)
second jobs—extra money
household maintenance and upkeep
dentists, orthodontists and doctors
lawyers, accountants, and taxes
voluntary work, service
poetry, art, and sensitivity to beauty
loafing—doing nothing for a while
meditation—time to think
charity and service to others
shopping

Too many things! It's hard even to keep them all in mind—let alone find *time* and thought for each. But aren't they all *good* things? Even television and loafing deserve a little time in a balanced life!

We have to look "beneath" these categories and then "subcategorize" them in order to separate the important from the unimportant.

For example, in the area of social relationships—friends and relationships are important, but gossip, small talk, and typical cocktail conversations usually are not. In the area of appearance and care of self, diet, grooming, fitness, and a whole host of other things obviously are important, but excessive wardrobes, primping, and preoccupation with style are not only unimportant but counterproductive. Shopping is necessary to a point, but wasteful (time- and money-wise) beyond that point. Second jobs when necessity requires them are "right," but when they indicate a choice of more material things over freedom and time with family, they are "wrong."

And then there is the question of timing. Lots of individual time with a child might be enormously important during one season of life and considerably less important at another time. The relative importance of various elements of life wax and wane during different life eras. The need (and desirability) of shifting emphasis between priorities was expressed clearly by a well-known feminist who surprised many people by deciding to leave the workplace for a period of time to have a child and to be with the child for his first years. Said she, "I still want to have it all—it's just that I've decided I don't have to have it all at once."

But even with good timing, *we need a manageable num-*

ber of things to balance. The problem with having dozens of priorities is that we can't remember them all, and we keep leaving things out simply because we forget about them. (This is especially true of "quiet" things that don't demand our attention—and some of our highest priorities *are* quiet.)

If we can reduce the things we are trying to balance to a small number—if we can categorize the important things into a *few* key areas—we can increase our chances of balance.

The best number of categories—the easiest number to balance—is *three*. It's relatively easy to juggle three balls, whereas four are many times more difficult. The mind can stay consistently conscious of three areas. With four or more, some are always overlooked or forgotten.

Lifebalance is best pursued when we set apart three priority areas. They are *family*, *work*, and *self*. The deepest and truest priorities of life all fit somewhere within these three categories.

Most people quickly accept family as one of the top three priorities. And work or career is such a daily necessity for most of us that it is also readily accepted. Women who choose to stay home with small children have the very challenging and important career of domestic management as the second of their three "balance points."

But many people question the third area. Should "self" be one of our three daily priorities—one of three points on which we balance our day? Doesn't that imply a certain selfishness or self-centeredness? Aren't there some other areas that are more important than self? What about service to others? What about prayer or religious commitments? What about relationships with friends or civic or community involvements or responsibilities?

If viewed correctly, the prioritizing or "self" does not *oppose* these things, it *includes* them.

Consider the following points:

· So very often, the best way to serve others is by taking care of ourselves and by changing ourselves for the better. We don't get to be better parents by changing our kids, or better friends by changing those around us. We become better friends and better able to serve others as we grow and develop within ourselves. Jesus Christ, to us the ultimate example of empathy, service, and sacrifice, was able to give us all that He did *because* He had perfected Himself. People must fill their reservoirs before they can empty them. We must gain gifts before we can give them.

· Just as we increase our ability to serve others by improving ourselves, so also we enhance ourselves by involving ourselves in service. Thus "self" and "service" are much closer to being synonyms than they are to being antonyms.

In other words, the old dilemma of "Am I doing this service to help someone else or just because I want to prove to myself that I'm a good guy?" is not really a dilemma at all. It can be both. It *should* be both.

Doing things for other people does make us better people, and it's okay to have their interest and our own improvement in mind at the same time.

· "Self in its most complete definition includes both the "outer" and the "inner." It includes the soul as well as the body, the heart as well as the mind. Self includes our character, our integrity, and our deepest inner thoughts.

The reason the third balance point is "self" rather than "other people" or "the church" or "public service" is that we are not in charge of other people or of the church or of the public institutions in which we may work. But we are (or can be) in charge of what we, ourselves, do for other people, or for God, or for various causes we may pursue.

We have stewardship or direct responsibility over ourselves, just as we have over the other two balance points of family and work.

In this context, there is ample justification for having "self" as our third daily priority. However, the preceding points do bring up one very essential clarification. It is that the balance point of "self" *must* have service as part of its definition.

When we ask ourselves, "What do I need today?" the answer, at least part of the time, should have to do with service—"I need to do something for a friend or neighbor." "I need to fill my civic or religious assignment." "I need to draw closer to God." "I need to help someone in need." "I need to be needed."

In other words, there is a necessity for balance within this third balance point. Some days we need something just for our outer or inner selves—like a nap, some exercise, a little time to read, prayer or meditation, etc. Remember that even very self-serving things can be done with others in mind—doing them will make you a better parent for your children, a better friend to your friends, etc.

Other days, our self-priority should be some kind of service, like making a call to cheer someone up or doing a church assignment or working as a volunteer. Remember that this kind of thing, while aimed at others, is still an important factor in what you as a *self* are becoming.

With this clarification, most people are able to agree that the three priorities of life that require daily thought (if life is to be balanced) are "family," "work," and "self." *The first step in obtaining lifebalance is to spend five minutes each day, before you write down any other plans or think about your schedule, deciding on the single most important thing you can do that day for your family, for your work, and for yourself.*

Even if nothing got done each day except the three key priority items—imagine the cumulative effect. In a year, over three hundred specific, clearly thought-out things would have been done for family, for self, and for work.

Remember that the key lies not in balancing our *time* equally between the three balance points (although each balance point does need some time each day), but in balancing our *thought*—mental effort. And thinking hard enough to establish one single priority for each area will cause the mind to stay aware of all three areas all day long.

By narrowing down and naming the three balance points, we begin to gain control. We can watch the three, now that they are defined, and stay conscious of them; we can be sure no one of the three gets too far out ahead (or too far back behind) the other two. Join us in deciding on the three—and in doing something about each of them every day.

3. HAVING A WELL-MANAGED MID-LIFE CRISIS ON PURPOSE

The much talked about, much feared, much experienced mid-life crisis is sometimes triggered by an event (a divorce, a career disappointment, a health problem). Other times it just creeps up on us, escorted along by advancing age, declining physical condition, increasing stress, evaporating belief that we will ever be what we thought we would be, or maybe by a gray hair.

Linda:

Upon finding my first gray hair, I began looking for wrinkles, too . . . and I found them. "Oh no! I'm getting old," I gasped to myself as I wondered how it would feel to look like my mother, who had just turned eighty.

I don't feel any older than I did ten years ago, but there I was at thirty-nine with proof in the mirror—getting older. For some reason it had never occurred to me that *I* could get old.

In the next few minutes, my life flashed before me. Then panic set in as I remembered our three-year-old daughter's answer to her grandma's thought-provoking question: "Saren, when will you be a grandma?" Saren answered with an everybody-knows-the-answer to that tone of voice: "When my wrinkles come out!"

On the spot, I decided that now was the time to think a little about the past and a lot about the future, but most of all to revel in the present. After all, another wrinkle would probably pop out tomorrow!

The results of mid-life crisis range from negative effects, like silly and dangerous attempts to regain the look and the feel of youth, to positive effects, like the reassessment of what is important in life.

A good illustration of the latter is former U.S. senator Paul Tsongas, who decided not to run for reelection because of an illness that threatened to shorten his life and because of his desire to spend more time with his family. Tsongas noted, in words similar to those of the old doctor quoted earlier in this book, that he had yet to hear of someone who said, on their deathbed, "If only I'd spent more time with the business."

Instead of waiting for a mid-life crisis to strike, how about taking the offense and staging a good early mid-life crisis for yourself, on your own terms, with the objective of making some reassessments and some priority adjustments *before* some event forces you to?

The best way to start is to mentally divide your life into seasons. One of the most quoted verses in The Bible tells us, "To everything there is a season." Think of your youth, your education, the beginning or "planting" of your career and your family as the spring. Think of the full "blooming," family rearing, career-advancing middle portion of years as the summer. Think about the rich late-career time as fall, when you may have the greatest opportunities to "harvest" your best ideas and biggest dreams. And think about the reflective, freedom-filled retirement years as the winter.

With these "seasons" as your framework, ask yourself what your priorities are for each phase of life. What are the things you will have unique access to and opportunities for in each season? (For example, ordinarily children come only in late spring or early summer, and raising children is usually over by fall.) Certain kinds of freedom and physical ability peak in the spring. Other kinds of freedom arrive with the winter. Wisdom and perspective and the related abilities to give public and private service are not fully unfolded until fall. And most people don't know themselves, or their world, well enough to know where they would fit best and contribute most until early summer (which becomes a very good season to stage an intentional, reorienting type of mid-life crisis).

Lay out your life like seasons. Decide what the priorities are in each. Ask yourself a lot of questions. Use your own knowledge of yourself and the suggestions in this book to find your own answers. This process, if it does nothing else, will make your life seem longer. (Segmenting, or dividing things into multiple periods, always does.)

We said in the first section that problems with balance result in part from having too many options—and too much freedom. The other side of that coin is that we are the first people in history who have enough alternatives and enough agency to actually design the kind of lives we want to live and the kind of people we want to be.

Doing so should be the reason for, the agenda of, and the objective behind the decision to have a mid-life crisis on purpose.

4. SUNDAY SAW SHARPENING

As a small boy, my favorite place was the University Woodwork Department, where my Gepetto-like Swedish grandfather taught. The airy shop had dozens of lathes, jigsaws, and other machines, all powered by the network of moving belts overhead. The room was always filled with the whine of the saws and the smell of sawdust. I was too young to operate the power tools, but I loved to *watch*—and Grandfather did let me build things with his wonderful Swedish hand tools.

One day he handed me a crosscut saw and a board. I tried to saw it in half, but the saw was so dull! I remember my right arm aching. I was sawing so furiously that smoke seemed to come from the board. But the cut lengthened very slowly. When I finally had to rest (the board less than one-fourth sawed through), Grandfather took his file and, in less than five minutes, sharpened the saw. I reinserted it into my little cut, and vroom, vroom, a few quick pushes and the severed piece fell away. What power, what efficiency, what a feeling of purpose and effectiveness. So much less physical effort and so much more result.

I remember Grandfather telling me that one good sharpening kept the much-used saw sharp for a full week.

In our busy, stressed, competitive world, too many lives operate something like this:

events and demands → allocation of time and thought → priorities

The demands on us and all the "things we have to do" control how we "spend" our time and thought. Over the years, the things we spend our hours and our efforts on become our working priorities whether we like it or not.

What we need is a way to reverse the arrows—to cause our true priorities to *determine* how we allocate our time and thought. Generally, this will modify and change the demands we make on ourselves and even alter the events around us.

The sawing analogy is so apt. How common it is to feel like we are working hard, busy all the time, tired all the time—yet not much is getting done.

Prioritizing and balanced goal setting *is* saw sharpening. A little time, set aside to think about what matters and how to go about the things we want to be about, can make all the difference. A good sharpening each Sunday can keep us sharp all week.

Richard:

There are some people who get things done and stay on top of it all through sheer endurance—through a high energy level and a low need for sleep. I am not among them!

I learned a long time ago (or was forced to accept the fact) that I'm a sprinter and not a distance runner. I can work hard and with intensity for a while, but then I need a rest—physically and mentally. I resented this fact for a long time—until I decided that life wasn't meant to be an endurance contest anyway. It was meant to be enjoyed. And changes of pace are essential to enjoyment. Rest or relaxation, or the times between the bursts of activity, are not wasted periods. They are often the times when we get our best ideas and when we see things (including ourselves) in the clearest perspective.

Those of us with limited endurance have a powerful need for lifebalance. We need to prioritize and we need to be efficient and effective in what we do. Most of all, we need to think more, because thinking can avoid huge amounts of unimportant exertion.

Sunday is the ideal day to "sharpen." It is the first day of the week and the best time to think about the other six. If you think of Sunday as a day of recreation, adjust your definition a little so it will read "re-creation of who you are and what you want to become." If you think of Sunday as a day of worship, remember that the greatest praise we can give to God is given by making something more of ourselves.

Think of Sunday Saw Sharpening as the organizing of dreams and the practical use of imagination. You will then find special meaning in Thoreau's promise: "If a man advances confidently in the direction of his dreams to live the life he has imagined, he will meet with success unexpected in common hours."

Thinking ahead, one week at a time, keeps our minds and our attention on what *could* be rather than on what Whittier called "the saddest words of voice or pen—'it might have been.' "

Linda:

After one of our long seminars on the importance of "Sunday Sessions," one woman bitterly complained. "I have no time to sit down on Sundays and plan. Do you realize what I have to *do* on Sundays?" As she ticked off all of her commitments and all of the detailed (and marginally important) things she had to do, everyone in the audience saw "personified" what we had been preaching all afternoon. In order to have time for our plan, we must have a selective plan for our time. Careful planning frees our minds to do the things we choose to do instead of letting it be imprisoned by all the things we have to do! It makes us realize that we can often be in control if we plan to be.

True, there are always children who *have* to tell you something, three-year-olds who flush stuffed animals down the toilet, children's arguments that have to be refereed, and telephone calls that demand attention. However, Richard and I committed early in our marriage to taking turns keeping the kids occupied and the noise to a low roar for a half hour each Sunday while the other had a Sunday Session—unconditionally and without exception. And that has made all the difference.

A half an hour set aside each Sunday—to ponder—to reassess—to jot down goals and schedules for the week ahead. People who are worried about their ability to do this kind of regular prioritizing and balancing usually have two concerns: First, they don't have time; second, they don't know how. Let's try to explore both excuses:

1. To say you don't have time to think and plan is like saying you don't have time to sharpen a saw. "Sharpening" is a time-*saving* activity. It allows us to get much more done, and to do it better, with less hassle.

2. This whole book is about *how!* Saw sharpening is an art and a skill (as was the way Grandfather handled his file). But it is a fairly simple art and it is learned by practice. Begin by setting aside a half hour each Sunday—the first day of the week—to look ahead and think about the rest of the week. If Sundays are busy, consider getting up a half hour earlier to have some thinking time before the business arrives. Saw sharpening is almost always more restful and more renewing than the half hour of sleep it replaces.

Whatever time of day you start your "Sunday Session," don't begin by thinking about all the things you "have to do." Instead, start by reminding yourself of your priorities and thinking about what you can do about them during the week ahead.

5. LIVING TO WORK OR WORKING TO LIVE

Ours is perhaps the only society in history where, instead of working to live, a vast number of people live to work.

Unfortunately, living to work doesn't necessarily mean that we love our jobs. But our work is a major part of our identity. When we meet someone, the first question asked is "What do you do?" For more and more of us, we *are* our jobs.

In other societies, work was the necessity—the means to other ends. People worked to feed themselves and to buy the time and means required to have access to more desired and more valued things—like education, or travel, or leisure, or the pursuit of music, art, poetry, history, or adventure.

So why has work become our preoccupation? Why, for so many, has work become the master and the manacle rather than the servant and the supplier?

Part of the reason may be that there are some very interesting and very pleasant jobs today. It's easy to guess why someone might get more excited about working twelve hours a day as a space engineer or an officer in an interesting and challenging company than his father got about his job as an assembly-line worker or a farm laborer.

And then there is our materialism. We have access to so many things, and all we need is the money to buy them. The more we want, the more we have to work.

But the real cause of our overorientation to work is the "norms" that surround us. Everyone works. People's identity is their work. It is very rare to ask questions like: "Do I really have to work?" "Do I really have to work *now* while I have preschool children at home?" "Do I have to work as long as I do? As hard as I do?" "Is there work that I might grow more from and enjoy more even though I might not earn as much and even though the job might not sound as good to other people?" "If I didn't work quite as much, what else could I do with my time?" "Are there some ways we could simplify and thus need less money?" "Is the real reason I work so much the fact that I don't really want to be at home?"

We don't ask these questions very often. Instead, we're fond of saying, "I have to work." "We both have to work." "We simply require two incomes." "It just takes more and more to live every year." "I have to be more specialized all the time to stay on top." "I only have time for my own field of expertise."

Do some thinking—your *own* thinking. Instead of going along with what everyone else is doing, figure some things out for yourself.

If you are a mother with preschoolers at home, add up the costs of working full-time as well as the benefits. Often women who think it through objectively find that 80 percent of a second income is used up in the extra costs of transportation, wardrobe, child care, and so forth. And this doesn't count the intangible costs paid by children who don't have the attention of either parent during their most formative years. Working and concentrating on small children does not always have to be "either-or." There are options like part-time and flextime, and you can find them if you want them badly enough.

Whoever you are and whatever your job is, watch yourself so that you don't do too much trading of freedom and time for things. Ask yourself if you really need those extra things, or newer things, or better things enough to give up more and more of the most valuable commodities of all, namely freedom and time.

Bertrand Russell's statement bears repeating: "It is the preoccupation with possession, more than anything else, that prevents men from living freely and nobly."

And Thoreau adds: "The true cost of a thing is the amount of what I call 'life' which is required to be exchanged for it immediately or in the long run."

Remember what was mentioned earlier: there are two ways to be financially independent. One is to have unlimited money; the other is to have limited needs. Many of our things are not only unnecessary, they are worrisome and time-consuming and freedom-consuming.

Richard:

We had one particular period in our lives that taught us a lot about what we didn't want. I was partner in a management consulting firm. Each week I had to spend one day in Boston, one day in Kansas City, and one day in Puerto Rico servicing clients. I was working sixty hours a week, eighty if you count travel time, a hundred if you count nights away from home. But I was making a lot of money and doing "glamorous" things. I was also losing touch with my children, running down physically, and missing a lot of things I didn't want to miss.

So we changed things. In my case it meant starting my own firm, working on my terms. For someone else it might have meant changing companies or finding a new field. We decided we could live on less. In fact, we decided we would live on 80 percent of what we earned, paying 10 percent to church and charity, and putting 10 percent into a hands-off investment fund. Living on 80 percent forced us to simplify and reassess what was really valuable and important. Investing 10 percent soon gave us more financial independence than what we had earlier when making more. And working to live instead of living to work gave me the time and the freedom to live the kind of family and personal life that I wanted.

National syndicated columnist Ellen Goodman put it this way:

> What of we who suffer from mid-life bulge, the years of small children and big career plans, when it's hard to keep any sort of juggling act in place?
>
> . . . There are times when we all end up completing a day or a week or a month as though it were a task to be crossed off with a sigh. In the effort to make it all work, it can become all work. We become one minute managers, mothers, husbands. We end up spending our time on the fly.

Linda:

I was in the back of a huge auditorium at the Pierre Hotel in New York attending a women's conference and listening to comments that amazed me. "The greatest need in America is for twenty-four-hour-a-day day-care centers so that women can leave children day or night to go to work."

Another speaker expected that the coming generation would have the luxury of "rotating families," where parents and children could readily move to "more acceptable circumstances" in a different family setting. "Computers will be preparing the meals at home to free the woman and enable her to spend more time in the workplace." "Equal salaries will be more readily available so that, at last, women can marry for love instead of money."

I could not help but wonder: Are we living to work or working to live? Our society sometimes dupes us into believing that our happiness revolves around our work, on how much prestige our job has, and how much money we make. In actuality, sometimes the most difficult challenge is working to live and making our lives work. Perhaps there lies the real prestige!

6. DON'T JUST DO SOMETHING, SIT THERE!

Linda:

I remember one specific autumn when I was trying to get our eight children to twenty-two separate lessons each week. Three took violin lessons, four took piano lessons, one had a 5:45 A.M. string ensemble group, four boys were playing basketball games twice a week each (thank goodness two were on the same team), one had a harp lesson and one a trumpet lesson, one was in a play and had rehearsals every night, two had dance classes, three had tennis lessons, and two had swimming. Another had to be taken to teach a lesson to a smaller child in the neighborhood.

I remember the distinct feeling that by Christmas I was going to be crazy. Rather than let it happen to me, I decided to just "sit there" for a while . . . analyze the situation and organize my cluttered, noisy mind. In only a few minutes I realized that (1) basketball season would soon be over, (2) I might be able to entice some music teachers to come to our home if I paid a little extra, (3) I could permit one small child (who wasn't enjoying it anyway) to quit piano, (4) I could organize a car pool for some lessons, and (5) Richard should be driving the boys to basketball.

Although there were times when I still felt harried—just those few minutes of thought were like a life-jacket being tossed to a drowning person, and I survived!

Think!

Humans have the capacity to analyze, to reason, to decide, to create, to think. When they do, they live in a higher realm.

But we do so too seldom. In fact, without realizing it, we often tell ourselves *not* to think. We say (to others and to ourselves), "Don't just sit there, *do* something." We somehow value action above thought. If we plan our days at all, we say, "All right, what do I have to do today?" and we make a list of what we have to do, what we're expected to do, what others have told us we should do . . . rather than what we choose to do and we want to do.

Real balancing goes on in the mind. And it begins to happen when we "just sit there" and think.

Richard:

I graduated from the Harvard Business School at a very opportune time. Business was booming and I had a dozen very lucrative, very promising job offers. So many, in fact, and so good, that the decision of which to accept was extremely difficult. Linda and I decided we had to get away and really think.

We went to Jackson Hole, one of our favorite places. We locked ourselves in a hotel room, which had a beautiful view of the Tetons, and we started to think. For two days we analyzed, not only the offers, but ourselves. What did we want? What was important to us? What relative importance should we give to where we would live, to security, to work environment, and so forth.

We took a piece of soap and made a big matrix chart on the wall-to-wall mirror in the room. We rated each job offer from one to ten on several different criteria. Finally, after really *thinking*, really sitting down and weighing and deciding about ourselves, we made a decision. It was not the obvious choice or the option we were leaning toward before the trip. But it was the right choice—and it was something we would not have realized was right for a very long time if we had not taken the time to think.

It's not only big decisions that deserve some sit-down time. It's also the everyday. Taking five minutes early each morning to ask questions like "What matters today?" "What can I do today for my family?" "What do I need for myself today?" "What do I choose to do today?" can make remarkable differences in how we live and in how we feel.

The key is to ask ourselves these questions *before* we start listing what we have to do—before we start writing down our normal schedule or routine.

The fact that most people do too little thinking is not due to a desire *not* to think; rather, it results from using up the energy that ought to go into thinking on other things.

Richard:

Part of our rationale for spending six weeks in the Oregon wilderness building a log cabin was my notion that, in the long evening hours, without the interruptions of telephone or television (or electricity or plumbing for that matter), I would finish writing the manuscript I was working on.

Instead, I learned something about how finite my energy was. After lifting logs and cutting notches with a chain saw for twelve hours, I simply had no energy left to think. I would sit down, pen in hand, and promptly fall asleep without writing a single word.

The lesson is that we need to put the thinking in front of the doing. Because if there is not time and energy enough for everything, we don't want thinking to be the thing we leave out.

We need to turn the phrase around and tell ourselves, "Don't just do something, sit there." Sit there for just five minutes *before* you live each day, and think about what you want out of the day and about what you want out of yourself.

7. MARRIAGE: SHARING AND SYNERGY

Marriage can be anything from a casual liaison of mutual attraction or convenience to a magical combination which includes "oneness" (1 + 1 = 1) as well as synergy (1 + 1 = 3 or more).

Synergy means a situation in which the total is greater than the sum of its parts. Sharing and communication combine with commitment as ingredients for synergy.

Linda:

At the time our parents were first married, very commonly the "theme song" for many marriages, from a woman's point of view, ought to have been "Anything I can do, you can do better."

By the time we were married (in the late sixties, during the heat of the women's liberation movement), the theme song for marriages seemed to be "Anything you can do, I can do better."

Now, for the happiest couples, the scales seem to be balancing at an ideal midpoint as many couples realize that the theme *should* be "Anything I can do, *we* can do better."

Many women have realized that what they need is not a "part-time employee" for a husband; that is, "Please, can you spare a minute to babysit while I dash out for the groceries?" or "Could you possibly pick up Andrew at his trumpet lesson on the way home from work?" What they really need is a partner! "How can we help each other raise these children?" and "Let's talk about how to make things work better around here."

When husband and wife truly respond to each other, not only as lovers gazing into each other's eyes but as partners looking forward together in the same direction, then the partnership is greater than the sum of its parts.

While synergy is usually a business word, the prime application for the concept is in marriage. Two people who live together, who communicate and share, who know each other's strengths and weaknesses, who love each other partly because of their similarities and partly because of their differences . . . two such people have incredible opportunity for synergism.

In the first place, they can decide who does what best, and organize their life together around a degree of specialization where each partner plays the roles and does the tasks that he or she enjoys most and does best.

In the second place, common, shared goals viewed from two separate perspectives become stronger, more attractive, and more complete. Life becomes a team sport rather than individual effort. And everything from accomplishment to beauty intensifies and grows as it is shared.

Richard:

We were in a seminar once where the speaker had several couples stand up and try to tell as accurately as they could what each other did during a normal day. We all found out how little we know about our spouses' life. Responses were: "Well, he goes to his office—he talks on the phone, he writes letters, I guess." "Aaahhh . . . well, I think she does the wash, or straightens up the house—maybe she watches the soaps." "I think what he does has something to do with the braking systems for railroad cars." "She helps people decorate their houses—goes with them, I guess, and picks out things."

The responses were all very general. We went home determined to know more about each other's day. The resolution led to a whole new way of thinking together.

Since Linda was spending most of her time at home with our preschool-age children, she became the "general partner" for what we started calling "the inner partnership," and I became the "general partner" for "the outer partnership," which included my job. We acknowledged that the limited partners in each case had as much at stake but spent less time. We started taking a few minutes each evening (usually in bed) to brief each other on each of the partnerships (general partner briefing limited partner).

> The result was not only knowing more about what each other did during the day—it was more help to each other, more *sharing* of ideas, more feelings of closeness, more appreciation and empathy.

We know some couples who hold an "executive session" together each week—an hour or so on Sunday where they work out together their schedule for the week and decide who will do what.

Others try to take at least one short overnight trip together each month, even if it's just to a downtown hotel, and to use the time to communicate, to reassess their goals, and to think about their own careers and futures as well as about the progress and development (and problems) of their children.

Synergy is produced in situations where two people support each other and consciously try to dovetail their abilities in working together. The support has to go both ways. Happily, our society is getting away from the notion that the wife's only role is to support her husband. A better perspective is that of mutual support and of the notion that what happens *outside* the home supports what goes on *inside* the home. C. S. Lewis said, "The homemaker has the ultimate career. All other careers exist to support this ultimate career." So however the "inner" career is shared or divided, the "outer" careers should be thought of as support rather than vice versa.

Richard:

Once, years ago, I came home from a business trip extremely excited about a novel I had picked up and was halfway through reading. I loved the author's imagery and description, particularly since the book was set in London, where we had lived for three years.

I couldn't wait to share it with Linda—literally couldn't wait—so on impulse I pulled the book in half (it was a paperback) and gave the first half to Linda while I kept reading the second half.

Since then it has become a tradition, one that shows terrible disrespect for books I suppose, but great respect for each other, and great desire to share.

Things somehow are not complete until we've shared them, talked about them, compared notes on them. Our library now contains a lot of books in two halves, held together by wide strips of masking tape. They are our favorite books because they have been shared.

We've also started to read out loud together, particularly when one of us finds a "heavy book" containing enough ideas or philosophies that you need to read it slowly (aloud) and with someone else who will discuss it with you and pick up shades of meaning that you would miss if you read it alone.

Many marriage partners *talk* a lot to each other but rarely *communicate.* Real communication needs to involve ideas and perspectives and insights. People who only talk about other people are essentially gossiping. People who only talk about problems, or each other's faults, or why the checkbook won't balance tend to lose respect for each other rather than gain it.

Reading together is one way of prompting communication about ideas. Balancing and scheduling together (as in a Sunday Session) is another way. The "five-facet review" discussed in the next chapter is still another. Hosting literary groups or discussion groups is another. Praying together is perhaps the best way of all.

Work at communicating more with your spouse about more things. Set aside time, schedule certain regular periods to talk, to work together, to brainstorm, to share. Use travel time and other routine moments together to plan and think collectively and to develop synergy.

8. PARENTING BY OBJECTIVE

Richard:

I had spent the better part of the day at my management consulting office with a small business owner who was having some problems. My first question (as with almost every client) was, "What are your objectives for your business?"

This man didn't know. He honestly didn't

know. With a vague, rather blank look on his face, he said, "Well . . . let's see . . . to make a profit, I guess."

I was astounded by a man who had a business but didn't know what he wanted for it or from it. "You can never manage something effectively," I told him, "until you have clear objectives."

That evening, we had an unusually rough time with our three small children. Linda just happened to say, "Why are these children so hard to manage?"

The irony struck me—truly struck me. I had spent the whole day telling a man he couldn't manage his business until he had clear objectives. What were our objectives with our children? I asked myself the question, and about the best answer I could produce was, "Well . . . let's see . . . to *raise* them, I guess."

If specific objectives are so critical to our third or fourth priority (our work), then they must be critical to our first priority (our family).

That night was a real new beginning for Linda and me. We began the process of defining our objectives for our children. The thinking eventually led to the writing of three books: *Teaching Children Joy* (a method book for teaching preschool children twelve different forms of social, emotional, and physical joys), *Teaching Children Responsibility* (methods for teaching twelve forms of responsibility to elementary-age children), and *Teaching Children Sensitivity* (techniques for helping adolescents to forget about themselves).*

We found that by having clear goals about what we wanted to teach our children at certain ages, and by focusing on *one* objective each month, we were able to *simplify* parenting and better measure or see just how effective we were at it.

Start off by forgetting the notion of "quality time" as a substitute for quantity time. It doesn't work. A parent who says, "I don't have much time to spend with my kids, but the time I do spend is quality time" is usually kidding him or herself. It's as though the parent is saying to the children, "Okay, kids, I've got five minutes. We're going to have fun now whether you like it or not."

Usually it is a quantity of unhurried, unplanned time that generates quality. And there is sometimes a need to simply set aside some time to just be with children, whether you can afford the time or not.

* *Note:* Further help with parenting by objective is available through the Eyres' "Teaching Children" series. There are four books in the series —*Teaching Children Joy*, *Teaching Children Responsibility*, *Teaching Children Sensitivity*, and *Teaching Children Moral Values*, all available from Ballantine Books.

Linda:

I lay in the hospital one summer with a broken ankle and crushed vertebra from a car accident and found myself caught up in the "if only" syndrome. If only I hadn't allowed a teenage friend to drive. If only we had left a little sooner so that we weren't in a hurry. If only I had yelled, "Look out for the soft shoulder!" in time.

Parenting can get us caught up in the "if only" syndrome, too. Luckily no one was critically injured in the car accident—but families can be critically injured if parents do not have some objective. It is so easy for the days and years to slip by without any specific objectives. We think we have plenty of time to spend with our kids, teaching them what we want them to know, when suddenly—it's all over. Unless we have been parenting by objective, all we have left is the " 'if only' syndrome."

The single most effective thing parents can do to improve the quality of the time they spend with their children is to have some idea of what they are trying to give to or teach to their children. To have, in other words, some clear and specific objectives.

Be careful as you set parenting objectives. Be sure you are setting goals for yourself in terms of what you want to give to your children. Don't set goals for what you want your children to be. Too often, parents decide they want a child to be a great artist or athlete or doctor or judge—without much reference to what the child wants or to what his or her gifts and attributes are. The notion of a child as a lump of clay that a parent can mold into whatever he or she wants is dangerous and damaging. A much better metaphor is that of a seedling, which, while it may be difficult to distinguish from other tiny trees at the moment, nonetheless possesses the potential to grow into a beautiful poplar tree. It will never grow into a great oak or a productive apple tree. The efforts of the gardener-parent should not be to change its species but to *learn* (by observing) what kind of a tree it is and then to nourish it into the finest poplar tree possible.

Richard:

We were living in London when our oldest son turned five. He was, in my mind at least, a basketball star in embryo. I had commented on the size of his hands and the quickness of his reflexes before we got him out of the delivery room, and I had put a basketball in his crib long before he had ever seen a rattle. The fact that he never showed any interest had not deterred me.

Now here we were in England, where no one played basketball. The boy was deprived. And I, as his father-coach, was not going to stand for it. I finally found out about an exhibition game between two American service teams on the other side of London.

The problem was that when we got there, I couldn't get Josh to watch the game. He kept gazing around, mostly *up*. I finally said, "What are you looking at up there, Son?" He looked at me, his eyes wide with excitement. "Those numbers up there, Dad. The ones on the outside keep going up by twos, and the one in the middle keeps going down by ones."

It was the scoreboard! The only way I finally got Josh to watch short parts of the game was by telling him that it was the ball going through the basket that made those two outside numbers go up.

What a lesson—for me. I committed myself to looking at and into my children, to try to see what was really there, rather than looking for shadows of myself or extentions of my ego.

Josh is now a computer-oriented adolescent, beautiful in his uniqueness, and different from me in so many ways, every one of which I appreciate.

Generally speaking, schools have a stereotyping influence on our children. They school our children rather than educating them. (School defined as "convergent learning," where everyone is supposed to come up with the "right answer," and educate defined as "divergent learning," where creativity is valued above conformity and where a child's good question receives more praise than his pat answer.)

Schooling may be the responsibility of the state, but education is the responsibility of the parents.

Remember the goal of balance as you set objectives for what you want to give to your children. Don't push small preschoolers into highly academic preschool situations before they are ready. They *can* learn to play the violin when they are two or to do square roots when they are three. But if they do these things at the expense of a real childhood or as an ego boost for parents who would like to boast about their "prodigy," then it is a deep and lasting mistake.

Books like ours (method books for teaching children various kinds of joys, responsibilities, and sensitivity) can be helpful in setting such goals for what you want to give your children and in having the methods and ideas necessary to focus on one objective each month. They can also help you with techniques for enhancing and developing your children's uniqueness. But there is something else that is even more valuable in the process of parenting by objective. We call it a *five-facet review*. It will help you to keep your child's life in balance and to arrive at objectives that are precisely right for your own particular and unique children. It works like this:

Once a month, take your spouse (or if you are a single parent, take a close friend or relative who knows your children) on a special "date." Go to a quiet restaurant together and limit your agenda to one topic—your children. Think about them one at a time by asking yourself five questions about each: "How is Jimmy doing physically?" "How is he doing mentally?" "How is he doing emotionally?" "How is he doing socially?" "How is he doing spiritually?" Discuss each question and make some notes. This will not require as much time as you might think, because most of the questions will need only brief answers: "Fine, no problem. Everything going well." But others will raise a red flag and you'll find youself saying, "There is something we need to work on."

Out of this five-facet review will emerge three or four specific goals for the month ahead—things you can focus on that will provide results you can notice.

This type of parenting by objective will not only help your children to do better—it will help you to feel better (and more balanced). It will also remind you that your children are your first priority—deserving in every way of your finest efforts. We all need these reminders in order to continually view our children not as irritations or impediments but as priorities, as chosen challenges, and even as privileges.

9. YOU OWE YOURSELF

The remarkable thing about doing things for yourself is that it is the most unselfish thing you can do. We all know that is true—when we stop to think about it. We can do so much more for others when we take care of ourselves. It is when our health is good, when we feel secure, when we are rested, when we are stimulated that we find the inclination and the insight necessary to help others.

There are two similar-sounding but drastically different questions we can ask ourselves. One, if repeated often enough, will produce within us jealousy, envy, insecurity, and perhaps bitterness and even narcissism. The other question, frequently asked, will lead to self-esteem, well-being, and to balance. One question is "What do I want?" The other question is "What do I need?" The second question is not only a better one, it's a *tougher* one. You have to remember which question you've asked and to be honest in answering. You have to avoid the trap of thinking you need what you actually only want.

The good question is often made easier and more clear by subdivision. Ask yourself, "What do I need physically?" (exercise? rest? less food? more food?) "What do I need mentally?" (stimulation? meditation?) "What do I need emotionally?" (solitude? the "pickup" of a little treat for myself?) "What do I need socially?" (interaction? new acquaintances? a quiet chat with an old friend?)

Get in the habit of asking the questions daily—then pick the thing you need most and do it for yourself that day.

Linda:

One year, when our children were very young, I became aware of how completely I was neglecting myself. I was caught up in the "martyr syndrome." It seemed that everything I was doing was for someone else, whether it was feeding husband

and children, neighbors and friends, running errands hither and yon, assigning food for the PTA carnival, or preparing a Sunday school lesson. After much frustration and contemplation, I decided it was time to do something just for me.

Thinking back over the years, I realized that one of my happiest times was when I was playing in a string quartet with three friends. I knew it would be difficult, maybe even crazy, to revive the group, because all of us now were mothers with preschool children and babies at home.

To my delight, I found that the others were as anxious to get back into music as I was, and with our common love for music, we prepared a concert with some children dancing in the background, some lying in our laps, some crying for peanut butter sandwiches, and a baby hanging on the cello tailpin.

The concert was a triumph in many ways.

One of the most obvious applications of the concept of balance is the taking of a little time and thought for yourself each day. It can refresh you. It can revitalize you. It can sharpen your perspective. It can send you back to the tasks of the day with more vigor and less resentment. And it can make each day more varied and more pleasant.

Also, in a way that is not fully explicable, it can increase your self esteem—your opinion of yourself—perhaps through the subtle suggestion that you are worth doing something for every day. As Churchill said, "We are all worms, but I have decided that I am a glowworm."

Finally, as discussed earlier, there is a predictable but seldom-discussed connection between doing things for yourself and doing things for others. After asking, "What do I need?" (and answering it), it is easier and more natural to ask, "What do others need? What can I give?"

Service, particularly anonymous service, can be exciting as well as fulfilling, and we seem more inclined toward it when we are taking good care of ourselves.

Do it! Form the habit of asking yourself what you need every day. Ask it once, don't dwell on it, but do something about it.

10. WHO DO YOU ADMIRE?

Admiration is an interesting quality. It can cause envy, jealousy, and discontent, or it can motivate and stimulate people to become more than what they are.

"Beware of what you want," it has been said, "for you will get it." Paraphrased, the saying could also read, "Beware of whom you admire, for you will grow more like him."

Whom do you admire? Whom do you envy? It's an interesting question, because in its answer we can learn a considerable amount about ourselves.

The answers to the question, on a general level, are

fairly predictable. In fact, they can be categorized into a fairly small number of groups. Many admire wealth, because they believe it can lend freedom and enjoyment. Many admire power; many admire fame. Professional athletes are often envied, as are acclaimed artists and performers, and corporate presidents and successful politicians.

It occurred to us not long ago that we knew a few people in these admired categories. And it occurred to us that it would be interesting to know whom *they* admire. Do they admire themselves? Do they admire each other (the other categories)? Or are they so self-satisfied that they envy no one?

Well, we asked four of them—the chief executive officer of a major corporation, a venture capitalist who has accumulated major wealth, an international sports star, and a well-known television personality.

The results were somewhat amazing, or maybe they weren't so amazing. *They all admired balance.* They each had their own way of stating it, but all of them essentially said they admired people who found time for the important things in life—for family, for relationships, for growing inwardly and developing their talents. Because of their own achievements and visibility, they see the relative unimportance of wealth, power, and fame and find it a little amusing that other people admire and envy them.

So for what it's worth, there's a little extra proof that balance is the most admired quality of all. It is what the "admired" admire.

It is as though we all have, without really realizing it, different levels of success in our minds. Someone who achieves wealth or position, recognition or power, is successful on one level. But someone who is secure within, who enjoys the love and respect of his or her family, and who manages to pretty well *balance* his or her life—such a person is successful by a higher (and deeper and more "inner") definition of the word.

One corporate leader, president of a major U.S. corporation, defined success as "nose prints on the window." What he meant was that you are a success if your children wait with anticipation for you to come home each night. He was in agreement with Mencius, who said, "A great man is one who does not lose his child's heart."

Inner feelings are a far better measure of success than outer appearances. Thus we are far more capable of evaluating our own success than that of others.

Discover and then enjoy balance in your life between work, family, and self. Then, while you may still notice those with more things or higher profiles, you will have the interesting, confident assurance that you have something too valuable to trade for any of it.

REVIEW: IMPLEMENTING PRIORITY BALANCE (WORKING THE TRIANGLE AND SHARPENING THE SAW)

Even if you agree with most of what is in these first ten "solution" chapters—even if you agree basically with all of it—there is no guarantee that it will change how you live or how you behave or how you balance in any significant or lasting way.

There just isn't any guarantee!

Change is difficult. Especially changing *basic* things, like how we use our time and how we "spend" our conscious thought.

Ideas are fun, and most of us enjoy reading things and thinking to ourselves, "Right on!" or "This is just what I need," or "These people are saying just what I've been thinking," but the stimulation provided by ideas or accepted suggestions is not usually the same stimulation required for implementation, for change.

Change rarely comes "naturally." Even if there's no debate at all about whether we should change. Implementation takes work—mental work. And mental work takes commitment. And commitment takes simplicity (chapter 1)—some simplified procedure or habit that gets at the heart of the change and can be specifically committed to and consistently worked at.

We said earlier that most unbalance is the result of bad habits. We get rid of bad habits most effectively when we replace them with new, good habits.

So here it is, the simple procedure, the new, good habit. (The problem with it is that it is so basic and straightforward that it may seem too simple).

But there's no such thing as too simple.

We call it "working the triangle." It's something you do for a few minutes *every day*. It implements and has impact on the suggestions in all ten little chapters dealing with priority balance.

First let's consider a triangle:

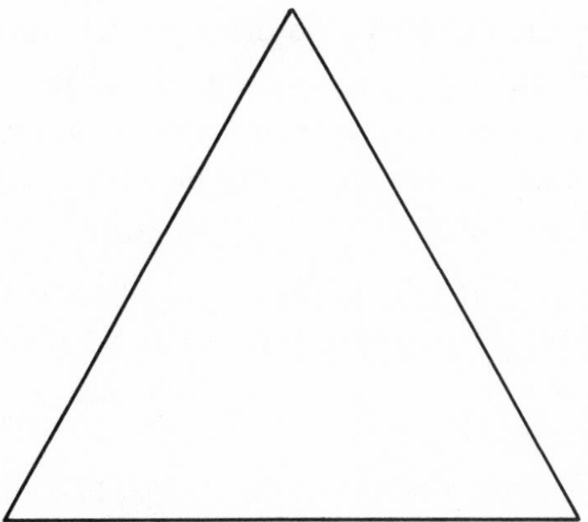

Three corners, each connected to the other two. No opposites. You can't crush it or skew it because each side holds the other two in place. There is stability because each corner finds its level independent of the other two and yet supports the other two. (A three-legged milk stool is solid on uneven ground.)

Now let's label the three corners with our three priorities or "balance points" (from chapter 2).

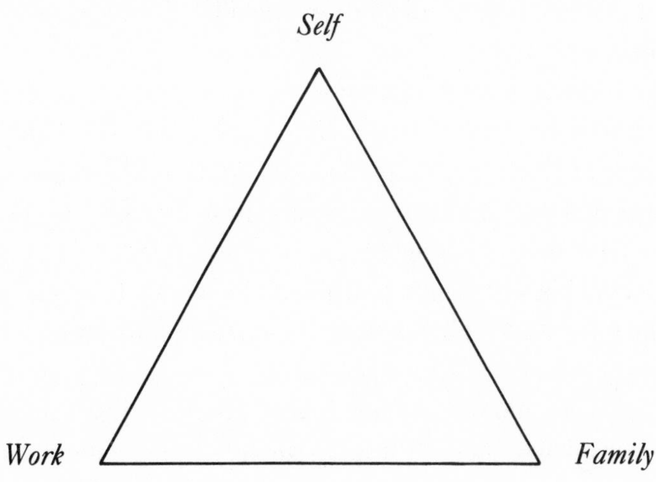

Each of the three corners balances the other two . . . and supports the other two . . . and draws from the other two. Think about the connections for a minute. We try to teach families the work and skills of achievement and the self-respect of service and responsibility. Our work and careers are for our families and our self-fulfillment and contribution. And the way we build ourselves and render service is through our work and through our families.

We've said all along that the danger lies not so much in forgetting that all three are important but in letting other, less important things get ahead of them or in allowing them to get out of balance with each other.

Balancing needs to occur daily. If we think about it once a year or once a month, or even once a week, we will look back and find we've been tipping—tilting away from balance a little each day so we can't get level again.

Daily balancing is accomplished by the habit of working the triangle every day—by setting one single priority each day for each corner. And by writing these three priorities down before any other planning or scheduling is done.

It's simple, but it's not easy. First of all, it's hard to remember to do it every day. And second, it's hard to think of the *one* priority for each corner. There may be twenty things we have to do at work in a given day. How do we choose the single highest priority? And how do we know what our family will need? Don't we have to wait and see? And isn't thinking of something to do for ourselves every day a little selfish?

Forget about these objections—they are just excuses, and we have dealt with them already in preceding chapters. The only thing that really stops us from setting these three daily priorities is our own unwillingness to spend the five minutes of thought that it takes to come up with them.

Each priority may be a little thing—spending some time alone with a child; taking a little time for yourself for reading, or exercise, or meditation; making a difficult phone call or working out a particular problem.

There isn't any other way. To be balanced, we need to think until we arrive at the highest priority for each corner each day. And we need to write them down. And we need to do them.

We need to "not just do something, sit there" (chapter 6) for five minutes each day—to think about each area, and about the demands, the situation, the opportunities of that particular day. Doing so may change just a little how we spend our time and how we live the day. But it also changes our habits of thinking. It trains our minds to consider and be aware of all three corners or balance points every day.

Whatever planner or schedule or list you use, whether it's an elaborate time management day-timer or a plain sheet of paper, start out by making three short "priority blanks" at the top for "self," for "family," and for "work."

Think of each blank as one corner of the balanced triangle. Ponder them long enough to come up with the day's three balanced priorities. This kind of mental work is hard, but it is not unpleasant. The "five-minute sit-down" may well become the most refreshing, most satisfying part of your day.

And the habit of *working the triangle* will become the key to your personal lifebalance!

There is a second habit, this time a weekly one, that

can make working the triangle more effective. Spend a half hour each Sunday sharpening your saw, or thinking about what you want to do during the week ahead (see chapter 4).

Use the three balance points of the triangle as your model in these Sunday sessions. Instead of thinking generally about your goals and dreams, think in terms of what you want to do during the coming week in the three areas of family, self, and work. Write the goals down, and use them as reference points each day when you work your triangle.

The weekly saw-sharpening Sunday Session also becomes a time to ponder the relative importance of family, (chapters 7 and 8), work, (chapter 5) and personal needs (chapter 9). It is also an organized, productive way to divide your life into balanced "seasons" and to have an intentional, positive, and ongoing mid-life crisis discussed in chapter 3.

The daily habit of *working the triangle* and the weekly habit of *saw sharpening* have the power to shove aside the habits of unbalance.

B. ATTITUDE BALANCE (BALANCING STRUCTURE WITH SPONTANEITY)

The second type of balance is *attitude balance*.

It is one thing to keep our priorities and responsibilities—the things we do—in balance with each other. It is another thing altogether to balance our actual selves—to create within ourselves the qualities of both discipline and flexibility, both structure and spontaneity; to develop an attitude that accommodates both the attitude of nose-to-the-grindstone work *and* footloose, family-free fun.

The society we live in seems to want us to choose between the two—to typecast ourselves as either fastidious or fun, either serious or silly.

Yet within ourselves, we know that to keep our sanity in an ever-crazier world, we know we need at least a little, and hopefully quite a bit, of *both*.

THE SOLUTION

The chapters of this section are designed not only to convince you that both attitudes are possible, but also to strongly suggest that, with balance, more of one can lead to more of the other.

11. JETS AND HOT-AIR BALLOONS

Is the objective to get there or to enjoy the journey?

Why do you get on a jet? The answer is obvious—"To get somewhere as quickly and efficiently as possible."

Why do you get in a hot-air balloon? Some may say, "Well, I don't—and I won't." (Remember you said that, because it's part of the point this chapter makes). Those who would get in a hot-air balloon would certainly not do so to "get somewhere." Because one thing that is certain about a hot-air balloon is that you don't know where you will get or when you will get there—and it really doesn't matter. It all depends on the wind.

So why do people get in them? *To enjoy the journey!*

Is there room in life for both jet planes and hot-air balloons . . . for both "getting there" and "enjoying the journey"?

Richard:

I took my young son on a hike one rare day. I knew it was important to be together, and he was excited. There was a plateau I figured we would climb to so we would have a level place to camp.

The first part of the hike was great. We talked. We enjoyed being together. But we weren't moving very fast. I started pushing him to walk faster. I got a little upset at our slow pace. I finally found myself carrying his pack and almost dragging him.

We made it to the plateau just in time to set up camp before dark. My boy fell asleep before I had the campfire going. When the flames grew and hit his face, I saw tearstains.

I realized that there are always two goals. One is to get there. The other is to enjoy the journey. Too much emphasis on one can ruin the other.

Jet planes and hot-air balloons are not the only comparison that illustrates the difference between getting there and enjoying the journey. We can set up a whole list:

jet planes	vs	hot-air balloons
get there	vs	enjoying the journey
swim upstream	vs	flow with the current
left-brain logic	vs	right-brain intuition
science	vs	art
structure	vs	spontaneity
discipline	vs	flexibility

snowmobiles	vs	cross-country skiing
outer	vs	inner
yang	vs	yin
motor power	vs	sails
planning	vs	serendipity
set plays	vs	free-lance
acting	vs	reacting (responding)

Most of us feel drawn to both sides of the list. We are made up of both the yin and the yang. We contain both the sensitivity of sails and the momentum of motors. We all want to get there and enjoy the journey. . . . And we know, when we think about it, that neither goal can satisfy us for very long without the other.

So often the reason people want to "get there" is that they believe getting there will help them to be successful or, in other words, "happy." But it doesn't work that way, and people who do get there often find themselves saying something like, "Is that all there is?" or, more philosophically, "I wish I had realized that happiness is in the journey, not in the destination."

If the journey is thought of only as the means to the end, it is rarely enjoyed, rarely appreciated. In fact, it is begrudged. We resent the journey as well as the time it takes us to get to whatever we think the destination is. So we don't notice beauty along the way, or opportunity, or needs.

Poets and songwriters as well as philosophers keep reminding us to live in the present, to stop to smell the roses, to appreciate our children while they're young, and to be aware of the joys of the moment. But peer pressure, advertising, and our own ambition keep nagging us to get there.

The instinct to get there is so strong in some of us that even our vacations lack the element of enjoying the journey. We plan every minute and worry if we're not at each new spot when our schedule says we should be.

By contrast, we have a friend who has had some of the greatest (and most adventurous) vacations imaginable with his family. They make a point of planning nothing and of concentrating entirely on the surprises of each new moment. They just get in the car and "go west" or "go east"—watching and waiting to see what each day will hold.

Linda:

I sat in the Atlanta Airport one afternoon and watched parents interacting with their children. The "movie" that surrounded me could have been entitled "Children Are a Useless Nuisance." One parent after another went by me, tugging on crying children, saying, "Don't touch that," in an irritated voice or yelling, "You come back here this *minute!*"

All were supposedly on their way to an exciting adventure (at least as far as the children were concerned)—to ride on a big airplane, or to meet Grandpa and Grandma—but the parents didn't seem to notice. They seemed irritated by the very presence of their children.

> Just the other day, while our three-year-old, Eli, was visiting at a grandma's and the older children were preparing a surprise birthday party for him, I was thinking how nice it would be when the house would be this quiet all the time as the children became older and able to take care of themselves.
>
> A few minutes later Eli arrived home. As the children popped out from their hiding places to shout "Surprise," and I heard the shrieks of delight and his funny "Yahoo!!" as he opened each present, I realized how silly I was not to savor every day with a child who would so quickly slip through our fingers and be off on his own.
>
> How difficult it is to appreciate the present and enjoy the journey rather than wish for the past or the future! Even through the routineness of life it is crucial to remember that memories are being made today!

You can categorize people, to a rather amazing extent, by the first thing they think when they wake up in the morning. There are the high achievers who bounce out of bed and say, "What can I accomplish today?" There are less positive but still very dutiful types who say, "What do I have to do today?" And there are the burdened, defensive people who essentially say, "I wonder what will happen to me today?"

But there may be a better alternative—a better thing to think with our first consciousness of the day. It is "What can I *enjoy* today?" "What are the challenges of this day? The responsibilities? The opportunities? And how can I enjoy them?"

The need, of course, is for balance. Someone who thinks only of getting there becomes an insensitive, self-driven robot, while someone who thinks only of enjoying the journey becomes an aimless, unfulfilled drifter.

The challenge is to remember that in everything, big and small, from a career to a vacation, from building a house to climbing a mountain, there are always two goals—to get there and to enjoy the journey. When we are conscious of both, it is usually possible to do both. And when both are not possible, we need to stop and think about which of the two goals is most important for that moment.

12. ANTIPLANNING

What we have today is the classic example of the tarnishing of a good name. In the name of "planning" we have an incredible proliferation of time management tools, executive day-timers, and exotic schedulers and organizing books. They're usually black or brown, but they have multicolored tabs and charts for everything.

The theory behind these planners, of course, is that they will help us get organized, help us be more efficient, help us get more done. And they do!

So why is it that the users and practitioners of highly

detailed planning and time management often seem to feel even more stress and frustration than the rest of us?

Because getting more done is not the answer. Balance is the answer. And most "planners" have a negative effect on balance. Consider the following:

· Ninety-five percent of what is written in planners has to do with work, career, or finance, so they are often destructive of the priority balance that should exist between work and family and personal needs.

· Planners cause us to live by lists, to act rather than respond. If we're not careful, our lists control us rather than the other way around. We begin to view things that are not on our lists as irritations or distractions rather than as opportunities, and we begin to lose the critical balance between structure and spontaneity.

· Because they are accomplishment-oriented, most planners focus our attention on things, on getting, and on *doing*, sometimes at the expense of people and giving and *thinking*. Thus they can be destructive to balance between achievements and relationships.

Lifebalance could be called "antiplanning" because it leads people in opposite directions—toward more emphasis on family, spontaneity, and relationships.

Balance and quality of life are not so much a matter of getting more done as they are a matter of deciding what is important and spending time and thought on things that are meaningful, whether they are planned or not.

"Planning" is a good and noble word, but it has been tarnished by the work-oriented, overly structured "time management tools" that end up being our rulers rather than our tools.

Richard:

In the small Idaho town where we spend part of our summers, there are still farmers who plow their fields with horse-drawn plows. The horses are fitted with "blinders" so they will keep their eyes (and their attention) on the furrow they are plowing rather than on the landscape, or the sunrise, or the female horse in the next pasture.

Highly structured planners and rigid "to do" lists are a great deal like blinders. They give us tunnel vision and focus us so tightly on our schedule that we don't notice the beauty, or the opportunities, or the people and the needs that are around us.

Antiplanning means throwing away the blinders of rigid structure and planned inflexibility along with the big, bulky, overly structured time organizers and day planners. It means realizing that the unplanned, even unexpected things in life are often more fulfilling than the calculated. It means enjoying rather than resenting the unexpected. It means setting goals (and even making lists) but remembering that the lists can be changed (or thrown out) if something more important or more beautiful comes along.

The term antiplanning also reminds us that setting goals and objectives is a very different kind of activity than planning and scheduling. Goals are the beacons and destinations that guide and energize our lives, and they should be clung to and committed to. Plans are our best efforts (at the moment) to figure out how and by what course we will get to our goals. The goal is not dependent on the plan. If we are alert and if we cast off our blinders, we will find better ways and straighter courses to our goals. One way to say it is "Be strong in your goals and flexible in your plans."

Most of all, antiplanning means a different kind of thinking that never allows work to supercede family or inner needs, that keeps people above things, and that spices the structure of our lives with frequent pinches of spontaneity.

13. FREEING THE MIND

Some people plan because they love details. Others plan because they hate details and want to get them out of their minds by putting them on paper—they want to free their minds so they can be receptive to beauty, to opportunity, and to ideas.

When do ideas come? Not when we're rushing, hurrying, worrying, scurrying; but on a beach, in the shower, driving, jogging, lying in bed, listening to a symphony.

The details of the day are dampeners and detractors to ideas. It is as though the mind has a certain number of circuits, and when most of them are tied up with schedules and situations, details and dates, few are left free for creativity, for ideas, for spontaneity.

Sometimes the mind is freed by routine or simple activity. Shaving or showering uses only a few circuits, and since we're getting something done, our mind does not pressure us as much to think or worry, so most circuits are free. If we're sunbathing, we're getting tan; if we're jogging, we're getting in shape; if we're driving or flying, we're getting closer to our destination—so our "achievement trigger" can shut down, the "don't-just-sit-there-do-something" syndrome can deactivate, and we can be more aware, more free, more open to ideas and insights.

Another way to free the mind is with a pen. Quiet the noisy mind by writing down the clutter, deciding which things you do when, and then forgetting about them until their time comes. Clearing the circuits is the best reason for list making. Too many worrisome details occupying the mind not only block creativity, they screen and darken awareness and appreciation and the ability to feel.

Richard:

Wiamiah Falls Park, on the windward side of Oahu in Hawaii, is one of the most breathtakingly beautiful spots on earth. Peacocks strut in lush, flowered meadows beneath massive banyan trees and below the cascading waterfall.

I sat one day near the path, back against a

purple flowering tree, and watched tourists go by, watched their faces, watched their eyes, tried to read their thoughts. All were thinking, "This is beautiful," but for some it was a small and quick passing thought, overshadowed by "bigger" thoughts, such as:

"How far is the waterfall; will I have time to get there and stay on schedule?"

"What should I take a picture of?"

"I wish the weather would brighten up; this would be prettier with sunshine."

"Where are those kids? I wish they wouldn't wander off."

"I better find a tour guide so I'll know what to look at here."

"I should have stayed with that jogging; I'm not in good enough shape to enjoy this hike."

"I wish Hilda would walk faster; she's always walking behind me."

"I haven't called the office in two days."

"I know there was something I forgot to do before I left home."

You can read the thoughts from the worry lines or the tightness of the mouth.

Awareness is the source of joy. Freeing mental circuitry is the invitation to intuition and ideas. Awareness is clouded by the same demanding details that clutter our minds and tie up our circuits. Get rid of them by writing them down. Carry a simple date book or schedule of some kind (altered by the priority blanks discussed in the last section). Use it as storage for everything *except* awareness of the moment.

14. SERENDIPITY

Horace Walpole, the English writer, enjoyed reading Persian fables. One day he read one called *The Three Princes of Serendip* (the ancient name for the island of Ceylon or Sri Lanka). It told of three young princes who went into the world to seek their fortunes. None found fortune, but each found something even better. One found love, one beauty, one peace.

Walpole was impressed by the notion of finding something other than (and better than) what was being sought. He felt a need for a word that could describe such "happy accidents" and (being a writer with license to coin new words) came up with *serendipity*. The full definition he gave to the word was "that quality which, through good fortune and sagacity, allows a person to discover something good while seeking something else."

Walpole would not like the changed and simplified meaning that today's world has given to his word. People who say serendipity is a happy accident miss Walpole's main point. To him serendipity was something that could happen only if a person was aware and sagacious and only if he or she was seeking something else which gave him or her a basis on which to judge something else as better.

Think about the implications of the real definition.

Serendipity is a quality that people can develop. It requires sagacity (awareness, understanding, observation, alertness), and it requires that we be seeking something (have goals, aims, objectives). The definition suggests that as we combine our sagacity with our structure, we will cause the phenomenon of discovering things that are better than what we were pursuing.

Richard:

There was a period during my college years when I became obsessed with positive thinking and aggressive goal achievement. I felt that the world was at my feet . . . that I could do anything if I had clear goals and plans.

I was totally preoccupied with accomplishing and not the least bit worried if what I wanted required the manipulation of other people. I don't remember any time when I felt so much in control (or any time when I offended more people).

My bubble was burst by a girl I was dating who, in breaking off our relationship, said she was sick of my goals and plans and would rather be with someone who was more spontaneous and fun. She also called me many names, among which "selfish," "insensitive," and "manipulative" were the nicest.

By sheer coincidence, our last date was to a concert by a group called "The Serendipity Singers." The next day, still dazed and reeling from the previous evening's criticism, I found myself wandering around in the library and, for want of anything better to do, looking up the meaning of this strange word.

"The quality of being aware and sensitive enough that you can find something good while looking for something else." What struck me was that I could have goals and be looking for something and still be aware and sensitive enough to find good things I hadn't sought, and relaxed enough to be spontaneous.

I adopted *serendipity* as my favorite word and began to think of it as my greatest personal need.

Years later, when our first child was born, I still thought so much of the word that we named her *Saren*. There aren't many kids who are named after a word! Actually, I wanted to name her Serendipity, but Linda worried that the kids would call her "Dipity."

I liked the word so much, in fact, that when our first son was born, I wanted to name him after the English author who coined the word. Linda said that she understood my sentiment and that she would have gone along with me if only the author's name hadn't been Horace Walpole.

How can anyone be so in love with a word? Simply because its real meaning is so marvelous and so meaningful. Serendipity can become a sort of bridge between regions that are otherwise hostile toward each other—lands which, without the "serendipity bridge," we have to choose between because the gap between them is so wide.

One is the land of structure and discipline, of goal setting, positive mental attitude, and achievement. It seems to be inhabited mostly by high-powered business executives, aspiring yuppies, left brain thinkers, and supermoms. The other is the land of spontaneity and flexibility, of sensitivity and observation and relationships. Here we find many artists and creative thinkers, philosophers and would-be Renaissance men, and people who use the intuitive right hemisphere of their brains.

People in one land travel in jet planes, power yachts, and snowmobiles. In the other land, many prefer hot-air balloons, sailboats, and cross-country skis.

Although there are overlaps, we generally associate people in each land with certain things: In the first land, people read the *Wall Street Journal*, dress for success, and listen to motivational tapes. In the second land, people read poetry, dress for comfort, and listen to Stravinski. In "Land A," politics means power, progress, military strength, and tax loopholes. In "Land B," politics means environmental conservation, peace marches, and compassion. In one land people live to work and say things like, "Act, don't react," and "Don't just sit there, do something." In the other land, people work to live and say things like, "Go with the flow," and "Don't just do something, sit there."

The problem most of us have is that we like both lands . . . and we like lots of people in both lands. And there are certain parts of us that we know belong in each land.

We require that each of the two has its own unique beauty and usefulness. We know that we appreciate one all the more after we have spent time in the other—like going from the snow in Colorado to a beach in California.

It is serendipity that allows us to move freely back and forth . . . even to have a home in each land.

Remember that serendipity requires sensitivity and highly tuned observation so that we don't miss things like beauty, needs, opportunities, and spontaneous moments. If we have this sensitivity and if we have clear goals and objectives (because serendipity only "finds something good" when "seeking something else"), then we have both the passport and the visa that let us spend all the time we want in both lands.

With serendipity we can live comfortably in one land because we are "seeking things"—we have goals, we want to achieve, to grow, to progress. But we can also feel at home in the other land because we have sensitivity and sagacity and are, therefore, flexible and spontaneous enough to change our minds and change our course when the right moment or the right need or the right surprise comes into view.

People who have cultivated the bridge or the passport of serendipity can find real fulfillment in meeting a goal, in checking off things on their "to do" list, in competing and in winning. But they can also feel the joy in a red sunset or in doing a spur-of-the-moment anonymous good turn, or in writing a poem, or in winning a small smile from a small child.

Serendipity is a bridge that lets us have our cake and eat it, too. We don't have to choose between being structured schedulers or flexible free-lancers. We can have both goals and surprises, both plans and spontaneity, both discipline and flexibility. We can ride in jet planes and hot-air balloons.

Serendipity is not luck, and it is not (despite its shortened definition) accidental. Serendipity is obtainable. It is a quality that grows in people who develop their awareness and sensitivity and their commitment to flexibility along with their ability to set goals and plan their time.

"Act, don't react," we are told at positive-thinking rallies and by "success" books. Be in charge, take control, decide what you want, and don't let anything get in your way.

What foolishness!

What an arrogant assumption to believe that we have total control over our own lives, that there will be no surprises, and that we can manage and manipulate all the things and all the people around us. And what a boring, unexciting prospect even if it could be true.

All we have hope of controlling is ourselves, and even that is a pretty tall order. With concentration and effort we can control what we want, what we pursue, how we live, and how we respond to the people and the world around us.

Well-lived lives achieve balance and develop serendipity as a bridge between acting and reacting, between controlling and responding.

A well-balanced day includes not only things you did because you had planned to do them, but unplanned things you did because you noticed them and chose to do them. For example:

- A father, looking out his office window, notices that

it is an exceptionally beautiful afternoon and decides he could finish the work he is doing now early the next morning. He goes home early and takes his three-year-old to the zoo.

· A mother notices that her third-grade son looks troubled and puffy-eyed as he comes in from school. She asks if anything is wrong and he bursts into tears. She decides she can get along for another day without grocery shopping and spends the next hour learning some very interesting things about some insecurities her son feels at school.

· A husband notices during dinner that his wife seems distracted, irritable, and cross with the children. He realizes it has been a while since they've been out together, so he forgets about the big game he'd planned to watch on TV, calls a baby-sitter himself, and takes his wife to a movie.

· A woman, hosting a social gathering at her home, hears the doorbell ring. Answering it, she finds an awkward, semiretarded boy who slowly tries to explain to her that he is selling magazine subscriptions. The woman, who is not interested in the magazines and anxious to return to her party, nonetheless notices that the boy wears only a threadbare, thin coat on this chilly night. She gets the coat her son outgrew last year from the storage closet and gives it to the boy.

· A couple, taking a weekend away for a sort of "second honeymoon," is waiting in a line in an airport to get a rental car. They strike up a conversation with a woman in the line, who happens to tell them of a marvelous, quaint little hotel. They change their reservations from the plan given to them by the travel agent and end up discovering a "perfect place."

· A businessman reads an article that gives him a new idea. He changes his schedule and makes some phone calls which end up providing him with a lucrative new client.

· A mother has set a goal to clean out her refrigerator, but just as she is starting, she notices that her two-year-old, for the first time she can recall, is looking at picture books of his own accord. She puts off the refrigerator for a while and reads to the child.

It is said that the archer hits the target partly by pulling, partly by letting go. Life needs to be lived partly by acting, partly by reacting, partly by initiating, partly by responding. It is as important to be sensitive to the needs of a child or to respond to a touching or beautiful moment as it is to accomplish a task or make a decision.

Reacting, responding, deviating from your plan to tend to something that just came up are not signs of weakness. Neither are doubts and questions; neither is a strong interest in people other than yourself and in fields of expertise other than your own.

Richard:

In some ways the years I spent earning an M.B.A. from the Harvard Business School were among the most exciting and interesting years of my life. I enjoyed the stimulation, thrived on the competition.

About halfway through the first year, however, I learned something about myself. I found myself feeling compelled to go "across the river" to the other parts of Harvard at least once or twice a week. I felt like I needed to rub shoulders with liberal arts and philosophy or history majors. I needed contact with people who were trying to understand the world, not control it. I needed interaction with people who asked questions instead of giving answers and still had doubts once in a while, even about themselves. I needed to mingle with individuals who carried paintbrushes or telescopes instead of attaché cases, and who wore jeans or lab smocks instead of button-down collars and blazers.

The problem with so many of my business school colleagues was that they were so bent on acting, on organizing, on solving, and on winning that they limited their world to what they could control and understand (which, by definition, leaves out the most interesting parts).

Serendipity is a remarkable quality—a bridge between lands that are otherwise unconnected. Perhaps the most amazing thing about serendipity is that it is so available. People who understand what it is and who consciously want it . . . find that they suddenly begin to have it.

15. AWARENESS, SUPERAWARENESS, AND GRATITUDE

Balance is largely dependent on awareness. Awareness, or "sagacity," as Walpole called it, is what triggers serendipity and reveals to us the unplanned needs or opportunities for which we should be willing to depart from our routine or our plans.

It is our awareness of the current individual situations of family members and of our own personal needs that keeps us working at "balancing the triangle"; and it is awareness of beauty and feelings and settings and moods that makes life interesting and joyful. Thoreau wrote, "Only that day dawns to which we are awake." Writer and philosopher Wilfred A. Peterson tried to list the qualities of awareness. Besides alert senses, he included:

· Identifying yourself with the hopes, dreams, fears, and longings of others, that you may understand them and help them

· Learning to interpret the thoughts, feelings, and needs of others through their words, tones, inflections, facial expressions, and movement

· Searching for beauty everywhere

· Knowing wonder, awe, and humility

· Discovering the mystic power of silence and coming to know the secret inner voice of intuition

Awareness expands our universe, expands our capacity, expands our abilities and our powers. Some have even said that the difference between man and God is a vast difference of awareness.

The mistake we make is in not thinking more about awareness. The more aware we are of awareness, the more of it we will have. The mind, in this instance, is an obedient subject. Tell it to notice more, and it will do so.

Awareness is not like hair—it's not something that either grows in our heads or doesn't. We *develop* awareness by conscious effort. And the very things we want to result from our awareness are the things that help us to develop it.

In other words, cause and effect can be interchanged. Just as it is true to say "The more aware we are, the better we will do at working the triangle and at having serendipity"—it is also true to say, "The more we work at balancing the triangle and having serendipity, the more aware we will become." Deciding every day on a priority for family, work, and self inevitably makes us more aware of ourselves and of the people, needs, and situations around us. Seeking of serendipity requires us to intensify our awareness.

Richard:

I remember one particular period of my life when I was struggling to "lighten up" a little. The stress of work and other commitments seemed so intense, and I felt like I was in a pinball game, bouncing from one task to another without looking up, without looking around.

One day, while waiting my turn at the barbershop, I happened to read a short article on (of all things) the virtues of writing poetry. "All poems start with an observation," it said. "Committing yourself to attempt a small poem on a regular basis will require you to *observe* and then to *think*. And these are the two things that awareness is made of."

I tried it and it worked. The type of thinking that it took to attempt a poem lifted me above the day's routine and brought about, at least for the moments involved, a new level of awareness.

In his remarkable little book, *A Guide for the Perplexed*, E. F. Schumacher divides the things that occupy this planet into four "levels of being": (1) "mineral" (matter without life), (2) "plant" (M + L, or matter with life), (3) "animal" (M + L + C, or matter with life and with consciousness), and (4) "human" (M + L + C + SA, or matter with life, with consciousness, and with self-awareness or the power to direct our consciousness in accordance with our purposes).

Schumacher then says:

> In a hierarchy structure, the higher does not merely possess powers that are additional to and exceed those possessed by the lower; it also has power *over* the lower. It has the power to organize

> the lower. . . . Are there powers that are higher than self-awareness? Are there levels of being above the human? . . . The great majority of mankind throughout its known history . . . has been unshakenly convinced that the chain of being extends upward beyond man. This universal conviction of mankind is impressive for both its duration and its intensity. Those individuals of the past whom we still consider the wisest and greatest not only shared this belief but considered it of all truths the most important and the most profound.

He goes on to point out that each level of being is profoundly more aware and more active (less passive) than the level below it. . . . But even at the human level a great deal of unawareness, passivity, and dependency remains. "Observing this," says Schumacher, "mankind has always used its intuitive powers to complete the process, to extrapolate the observed curve to its completion. Thus we conceive a being, wholly active, wholly sovereign and autonomous; a person above all merely human persons. The four levels of being are thus seen as pointing to the . . . existence of a level (or levels) of being above 'the human.'"

A higher awareness exists which can enlighten and expand our own awareness and produce the "flashes of insight" to which most scientists and "discoverers" attribute their clearest understandings. Whether it is categorized as a religious belief or simply as a sense of some source of insight and awareness beyond our own . . . regardless of our personal terminology or perspective . . . two conclusions can be drawn:

1. It is there.
2. We can tap into it.

This superawareness can help us see more sharply what is important and what simple things we could do to make a difference. And it can help us discover serendipity through a flash of insight or a new idea, or the "noticing" of an unpredicted opportunity or need.

How do we tap in? How do we increase the "frequency of our flashes" and expand our own awareness beyond the data given to us by our five senses?

The answer is both so simple and so logical that it is easy to overlook. The answer is to *ask*.

The most frequently repeated admonition, both in biblical Scripture and in writings of other world religions, is the admonition to ask.

Whether a person has a clearly defined idea of God or an extremely vague idea of some higher awareness, it stands to reason that the greater comprehends and has interest in the lower . . . and will respond to the lower's request for expanded awareness.

Ask for expanded awareness. Ask whoever you conceive the possessor of that greater awareness to be, or ask the awareness itself. Make the request as you sit down to work your triangle and decide on your three priorities each day, and ask it in your mind as the day unfolds and as you strive to notice the unplanned and the unexpected.

With awareness (and more especially with "superawareness") comes gratitude. Awareness of beauty, awareness of love and tender feelings, awareness of the meaning and value of difficulties and challenges—all true awareness leads to gratitude.

Richard:

In our family, we have come to think of gratitude as such an important quantity that Thanksgiving has become, in many ways, our favorite holiday. One tradition we have is to make a list each Thanksgiving morning, on a long roll of cash register paper, of everything we can think of that we are grateful for. (Last year we listed over seven-hundred things.) Then we have time contests to see who can read through the whole list fastest.

We have also adopted the tradition of sending out a family Thanksgiving card each year instead of a Christmas card. It always contains a current picture of our family along with a poem.

Gratitude can and should be cultivated. It is not only a product of awareness—it is a precipitator of awareness. As we learn the art of gratitude, we become more aware.

The interchange between awareness and gratitude can extend to a deeper sensitivity to our relative position in the world and can make us grateful even for our problems.

Linda:

One morning I woke up feeling that my mind was in a vise. How am I going to survive this day? I thought. I have to help the children while they practice, grab the boys before they get out the door without combing their hair, and write notes to teachers. I have to take a child to the dentist, get one child to work after school, and another to a harp lesson, and another to Cub Scouts. I have to finish some writing for a newsletter, find someplace to put my preschoolers while I give an art lesson to the sixth grade for the PTA, fix dinner for ten, and speak at a meeting. Then, after all that, I have to go to the airport and pick up a "new member of our family"—a twenty-two-year-old university student from mainland China whom we had agreed to sponsor.

Somehow I survived all the "have to's" for the day. The next twenty-four hours with this young girl from another world taught me an important lesson which freed my mind from much of its stress. She told us that she had been assigned an occupation according to a test she had taken—also that families were limited to one child, whom the mother is allowed to stay home with for one year before she returns to the factory and puts her child in the factory nursery. This young lady's "upper-class" family shared a living room with another family and were not allowed to plant a tree without government permission.

Suddenly all my "have to's" became "choose to's." I acknowledged that I had chosen my family size and my hectic schedule and demanding commitments. And I could choose to eliminate much of it—if I wanted to.

The next morning, as I rolled out of bed, I was so grateful that I was in charge, and I realized that I love my problems!

Decide to be more aware and to be more grateful. Work on it in your family and in your own mind and heart. Use a pen to help you—write poetry about your awareness and diary entries about your gratitude. And return thanks to the source of superawareness, even as you ask that source for more light and for more sight.

16. THE SPEED OF GOING SLOW

One heroic character we remember from comic books had the power to slow time down—so that everything and everyone around him was in slow motion—so that he was the only one who could move fast. In this situation he could speed past opponents to score or win in any sport, he could easily block any attack on himself, he could even catch bullets in midair.

A lot of us wish for something like that. And since we can't slow things around us down, we try to speed ourselves up. We *hurry*, we rush, we hustle. We run ourselves ragged trying to get ahead . . . or to stay even . . . or to catch up.

And then occasionally we run into one of those puzzling individuals who seem to have time for everything, and for everyone. He doesn't hurry. He doesn't seem impatient or rushed. It almost seems like he's got nothing to do. . . . Yet he gets so much done!

Think about something: Stressed people are always in a hurry. People in a hurry are always stressed. People who don't hurry aren't frustrated. People who aren't frustrated don't hurry. Which is cause and which is effect? Does hurry cause stress or result from it?

Now think about something else: People who are in a hurry never have enough time.

Could it be that we are more like the comic-book character than we think? Could it be that our attitude and our approach to life actually affect how fast time passes for us? Perhaps we are a little like mice on a treadmill who, by running faster and faster, succeed only in making their world spin around them faster. And perhaps, conversely, when we relax, when we consciously slow ourselves down and become a little more patient, a little more observant and sensitive—perhaps then we actually slow time down and find ourselves able to do more by hurrying less.

One thing is for sure. When we slow down and center ourselves, we begin to see more; and part of what we see may be a shortcut, or a better way, or even a better place to be or a better thing to do. We begin to think more when we slow down, and thinking usually saves time. We begin to be more aware of what is really important. And we start to notice what is unimportant—enough that we can abbreviate it or even eliminate it.

One year, a part of our family Thanksgiving card was about the speed of going slow:

Can words describe this sense, so seldom obtained?
So soft, so simple.
Time for people, inner peace enough
to look into eyes with interest—instead of self-
consciousness
Time to wait—and let things come to you instead
of going after them.
More time, slower time.
The curious calm capacity to enjoy simply,
to think freely, to feel deeply.
A slow, sweet sensation, a stillness inside.
You feel the ground through the soles of your shoes
and the sky all around you.
A feeling like ripples, gentle and easy across vast
depth.
Sometimes it comes after a catharsis,
after four or five days of vacation,
trying to relax, finally slowing down,
Sometimes it just comes, unexpectedly, perfectly
for no apparent reason except
maybe you slowed down, looked around,
liked what you saw
or maybe you asked for it, believing that it can
come as a gift
from a spirit far deeper than your own.

Linda:

For Mothers Day last year the children gave me a treasure. Our fourteen-year-old, a gifted artist, had drawn a characterization of each family member, and above each head was a little balloon (cartoon-style) with that person's most common "saying." All the children had helped to fill in the balloons.

The comments ranged from "I'm telling" above the head of our ten-year-old tattler to "I'm not your little servant!" above the head of our three-year-old (which he says every time anyone asks him to do anything). Apparently they could not limit themselves to just one comment from me, because above my head were four little balloons containing the following sayings: "Where are your shoes?" "Where is my purse?" "Practice!" and "Get in the car; we're late!" (Notice there was nothing like, "Come here, you sweet little thing, and let me kiss you.")

It was that fourth balloon above my head which struck me most forcefully. I pride myself on being on time, and yet when I start hurrying and get hassled, I get irritable, I say things I don't mean, I break things, I back the car into posts, and generally become hard to be around. The children's message inspired me to set a goal for the next month—a goal to slow down—even if it caused me to be late for a few things. With the goal in mind, I succeeded in slowing myself down and was amazed at how often I got more done and arrived early for commitments.

That and other experiences like it have convinced me that there is a "speed" in going slow. It is still a struggle to keep myself from pushing kids out the door and yelling, "Get in the car; we're late!"—but I'm working on it.

"Slow down, you move too fast. You've got to make the morning last," says the "Fifty-Ninth Street Bridge Song." Other songs tell us to "take time to smell the roses" and to live in the present—to live "Today while the blossom still clings to the vine." The lyrics reach us somehow—touching some inner place in us that knows that hurry never works and that we miss so much if we move too fast. Another song, from the Roger Miller score of Broadway's *Big River,* warns against becoming one of "the hasty hard to know" and advises us to "just lie and let your feelings grow accustomed to the dark, and by mornin's light you just might know the feelings of the heart."

When we teach ourselves to slow down, we are also teaching ourselves to feel more, to notice more, to be more sensitive and tuned in with other people. The slowdown brings with it a contagious calm. We find our children magically more peaceful, easier to manage, and inclined to give us spontaneous kisses and hugs.

Richard:

We've only bought three video movies in our life. Videos cost too much, and who would want to watch a movie over and over anyway?

I didn't think the three we have purchased had anything much in common with each other until I happened to think about them while we were writing this chapter. They are *Chariots of Fire, The Black Stallion*, and *The Man from Snowy River*.

We bought them because we sensed that they each had something to teach our children—something in their tone and their feel that we wanted for more than one evening. Without really thinking about it, we assumed that that "something" was probably a good moral or a clear portrayal of values.

But we realize now that it's something beyond that. Each of the three movies portrays a certain calm, and takes the time to focus and dwell on the beauty of the moment. The lead character in each film is patient and peaceful, able to think and reflect and observe—to respond calmly to whatever challenge arises. The tone in each case is the opposite of hurry.

Slow time down by slowing yourself down. The more you succeed in doing this, the longer your life will be.

17. PLAYFULNESS AND HUMOR

"The reason angels can fly," said G. K. Chesterton, "is that they have learned to take themselves lightly." Most of us have not learned to take ourselves lightly at all. As a result, we are a lot less like "the angels" than we are like Woody Allen's self-description. "Most of the time I don't have much fun," said Allen, "and the rest of the time I don't have any fun at all!"

Linda:

One morning I stomped into the kitchen while all the children were sitting at the breakfast table. I was absolutely furious about how the day had gone thus far. Absolutely no one had done absolutely anything they were supposed to have done. No beds were made, no practicing was done, and these chattering little "good-for-nothings" dared to be giggly at the breakfast table as though it were just another day!

Smoke must have been curling out of my ears as I, pregnant and hormone-laden, began yelling at the kids—uncharacteristically loud and menacingly. Some looked shocked, others amazed, one maybe even a little frightened. But one with big brown eyes and a grin on his face began to giggle.

"Noah, don't you *dare* laugh at me when I'm

this angry. You're taking your life in your hands!" I screamed. Seven-year-old Talmadge leaned his head over on ten-year-old Saydi's shoulder and began laughing, too. It was as though someone had turned on the laughing gas. They were all tittering—as though they were watching a funny movie.

After a few moments of blinding truth, I realized that they *were* watching a funny movie—starring ME! It wasn't easy, but I took one step back and looked the situation over and managed to crack a smile and a little giggle myself.

We all know that the old formula, crisis + time = humor, is true. In hindsight I'd like to add that the shorter the time element is, the better . . . for everyone's mental health.

Life in a crisis-ridden existence can certainly be lighter and funnier and more enjoyable if we look at the world not through rose-colored glasses but through humor-tinted glasses.

Having fun, taking ourselves lightly, playfulness, humor. How important are they? We're told by doctors that laughter is the best cure for ulcers. A good laugh, it seems, secretes a chemical in our stomachs that aides digestion. Dr. Norman Cousins claims with great credibility that he cured his cancer with a regimen of laughter (which, among other things, involved watching videos of old Laurel and Hardy and Three Stooges movies).

Humor and playfulness not only refresh our own sense of perspective and aid our health and well-being, they also have an obvious positive effect on others. They cheer people up and take their minds off their troubles.

Richard:

Our nine-year-old son, Jonah, has said for a couple of years that he wants to be a doctor. (His desire stems partly from the friendship he's developed with our family doctor through having been stitched up and put in casts so many times. Jonah is so interested in the process that he's almost pleased when one of his frequent injuries occurs.)

The other day I asked him why he thought he'd be such a good doctor. "Well," he said, "for one thing, blood doesn't make me sick at all! And for another thing, I'm pretty good at telling jokes, so I can keep people's minds off their hurts."

Someone who has a goal of smiling more will suddenly find the people around him smiling more, too. Fun is not a childish pursuit—but it is contagious.

Humor is related in a most interesting way to service

and empathy. Each of the qualities depends on observation and awareness. People who are empathetic and centered are able to be that way because they observe and see clearly the situations and needs of other people. Humor also comes from awareness—from noticing the little ironies and quirks of life—and from seeing the universality of the human predicament. Next time you listen to a stand-up comedian, realize that he's talking about very ordinary things which he sees in an extraordinary and perceptive way. In this sense, humor is also related to poetry. Both the comic and the poet see things in ordinary life that the rest of us miss.

Somewhere inside us, we all want to be more playful—and we know that the playfulness is in us . . . somewhere.

Richard:

I was lecturing at a large insurance association seminar. The speaker who preceded me was a nonconformist type of fellow whose subject was "having fun." He came into the hall (where everyone was wearing business suits) in a pair of cords and a lumberjack flannel shirt. He started out his presentation by asking "All right, what do you people do for fun?" After a short, awkward silence, a couple of men raised their hands. One played tennis, but as the speaker questioned him, it became obvious that tennis was a very competitive ego thing for him, and not much fun at all. In the meantime, the second man pulled his hand down.

After it had become clear that the audience really didn't do much of anything for fun, the speaker started telling us all what he did. He always paid for his car *and* the car behind him at highway tollbooths so he could watch in his rearview mirror the drama that unfolded when the driver behind him was told that his toll had been paid. He sent his favorite cartoons from *The New Yorker* to friends whom the cartoons reminded him of. When he traveled, he put little stick-on gold dots on airplane window panes or on public phones or rest room mirrors as a little game with himself so he would remember that he had been there before if he ever got there again. Whenever he boarded a crowded elevator, he waited until the door closed and then turned to face the people and said, "You're probably wondering why I've called you all together here today. . . ."

Since I was the next speaker, I was seated on the stand, watching the audience. Their faces showed a mixture of dismay and admiration. They didn't really want to be impressed with this sort of craziness and nonsense, but they couldn't help being intrigued, and at least a little envious of someone who was simply having a lot more fun than they were.

The seminar was in British Columbia, and it

happened that I had an extra day before my flight home. I was influenced by the "lumberjack"—enough that I used the day to go fishing. I kept the biggest fish I caught—froze it, wrapped it in plastic wrap, and carried it home in my briefcase. On the plane, I found I was even more influenced by this idea of playfulness than I had thought. A very bored stewardess came by with her nasal, canned voice, saying, "Sir, would you prefer the brazed tips of beef or the chicken cordon bleu?" Without stopping to think, I opened my briefcase and said, "Neither, actually. I detest airline food, so I bring my own. Would you please cook this for me?"

Besides making us more alive, curing our ulcers, and making people around us happy, playfulness is a great way to escape boredom. Speaking of tollbooths, we are reminded of a day crossing the Bay Bridge between Oakland and San Francisco. Thirty-seven of the thirty-eight tollbooth attendants operated like machines, taking money, giving change, sometimes saying "Thank you," for eight hours straight. The thirty-eighth tollbooth attendant was having fun. He had his boom box playing, and he practiced tap dancing (and sometimes singing) between cars.

"But I'm not funny, I'm not playful," you say. Well, why don't you be? It's your choice.

18. IS ANYONE TOO SPONTANEOUS?

For every person who has become too structured and allowed planning to take away his or her flexibility—there is another person who has far too little discipline, who is being simply swept along by the currents of life, seldom if ever setting a goal or preparing a schedule.

Richard:

We had been giving *Lifebalance* Seminars for over a year, mostly to corporate and professional groups and almost exclusively to the type of yuppie overachievers who needed the spontaneity-serendipity-relationships emphasis of lifebalance. Our audiences were too aggressive, too structured, too married to their work—and most of them knew it.

Then one pleasant week we flew to Hawaii to present *Lifebalance* to a large group of Polynesians. Luckily our format involved lots of audience participation. If it hadn't, we probably would have gone right on preaching flexibility and antiplanning and taking-time-for-fun to people who had never set a goal or made a list in their lives!

The situation started becoming clear to us when we asked, "How many of you use some kind of time management tool or planner?" and fewer than a dozen people raised their hands (out of five hundred). It really became clear when a man on the back row said that he thought a time management tool was some kind of an extra-fancy socket wrench. It was an interesting afternoon. As it developed, we found that most of these people did know what planners were but couldn't imagine why they (or anyone) would use one.

"You do what needs to be done at the moment" was their attitude, "unless there's nothing that needs to be done badly, and then you do whatever you want."

"But what if there are so many things that need to be done that you don't have time to do them all?" we asked.

They looked at us, looked at each other, shook their heads a little—trying to understand what in the world we were talking about.

That day we took a whole new approach to lifebalance. We ended up trying hard to convince the audience that there was some value in setting a few goals and promising everyone there that the lifebalance method would allow them do so *without* taking away their spontaneity or their wonderful ability to live in the present.

For some, setting no goals and making no plans is simply a matter of culture. For others, it is a matter of laziness. Still others avoid goal setting out of a conscious fear of responsibility. But for many, it is a matter of choice based on a decision to value spontaneity and flexibility and not to kill either with too much structure.

Richard:

We frequently open *Lifebalance* Seminars by asking our audience how many use time management or planning books. Lots of hands go up, and normally about half of the audience is anxious to tell how much they depend on their planning system and how much it has done for them.

Then we ask how many intentionally *don't* use detailed planners, and why. We ask what the potential drawbacks and disadvantages of these tools can be. And it is like opening a floodgate.

The other half of the audience suddenly has something to say. "Lists and planners take away your spontaneity." "They set you up to fail." "They make you worry." "They make you stiff and insensitive." "They cause you to be too aware of all the things you should have done."

Most people have come to think of it as an either-or question. Either you schedule and structure everything and make yourself into a machine, or you stay free and spontaneous and sensitive.

Getting both sides from the audience sets the stage for us to explain lifebalance . . . to try to persuade half of our audience to adopt serendipity and be free from their schedules once in a while . . . and to persuade the other half that daily goals and priorities can be set in a balanced way and be *combined* with awareness and sensitivity.

Remember that the goal is balance. At the heart of balance lies the understanding that a little structure is good for spontaneity—and a little flexibility is good for discipline.

19. WHEN, THEN OR NOW?

Goal setters tell us to project ourselves into the future. Poets tell us to live in the present. Genealogists and historians extol the benefits of the past. How should you orient your life? Is it best to live in the future, the present, or the past?

Be careful; the question establishes another dangerous set of false alternatives, another choice we should *not* make another time when we are wisest to choose the answer "all of the above."

The past, the present, and the future are not opponents or competitors; they are teammates. They are different generations of the same family; they are interdependent cogs in the same machine. And they can be great friends—friends that assist each other, learn from each other, and teach each other.

Linda:

I remember thinking one day when our first child was nearly a year old, "Won't it be great when this child can walk? . . . I'm breaking my back carrying her everywhere."

Saren was one of those children who learned to walk all of a sudden, and just a couple of weeks later I caught myself saying, "Wasn't it great when this kid would stay in one place!"

The "Won't it be great?"/"Wasn't it great?" syndrome affects all of us to some degree. The medicine for it is not to quit thinking about the future or the past, or even to quit thinking about how wonderful they will be or were. The medicine is to add, in the same breath, how great (or at least how interesting) the present is also.

Instead of longing for the good times of the past, be content simply to remember them with relish. Instead of longing for the future to come, enjoy the process of planning how you want it to be. Learn to see the present as that one focused moment when you can actually do things rather than remembering them or planning them.

The fact is that you can live in the future, the past, and the present all at once. The best way to learn how to do so is to get three books of blank paper. Label one of them "the past," and use it as your diary. Whether you write in it daily, weekly, or just periodically, concentrate on things you have learned, things you have felt, and progress you have made. If you've never kept a diary before, try to catch up by dividing your past life into eras separated by major changes, moves, or milestones in your life. Then write (or tape-record and have it transcribed) everything you can remember about each era.

Label your second book "the present." Use it as a way to enhance your awareness of "the now." Write poetry or short essays about your observations, about beauty or particular intrigue you have noticed, about your experiences of the moment.

Call the third book "the future," and use it to plan the future eras of your life—to set goals for who and where and what you want to be at certain dates that lie ahead.

Linda:

I thought that what I wanted more than anything in the world was another driver in our family—someone to help me get everybody where they were supposed to be during the week. I counted the days until our oldest daughter turned driving age the way a child counts the days until Christmas.

We turned her over to a driving school to get the required certificate to apply for a license. A few days before she took her driving test, I went out with her. To my horror, I realized that she was unsafe at any speed.

Finally on our test drive she said, "Mother, if you gasp for breath one more time, I am going to scream. You are making me soooo nervous!"

She did get her driver's license—much to my amazement. But her first time out alone, I couldn't help thinking . . . "What if she goes off the road or doesn't see a car coming? And there I was again saying, "Wasn't it nice when I didn't have to worry about this!"

Learn to live simultaneously in the past, the present, and the future, and think of the three as friends of yours as well as friends of each other.

Think of yourself as a mountain climber. Enjoy looking up at the peak you intend to climb. Enjoy looking back at the view of where you've been. And enjoy the feel of the rocks through your soles as you take each step through the present.

20. TAKING RISKS AND FOLLOWING FEELINGS

We know a tennis instructor who is always saying to his students, "Take risks! You won't hit many winners," he says, "unless you go for it and risk hitting the ball out. And the real joy in tennis is not winning, it's hitting winners."

Life is much the same. Avoiding risk, never trying anything we are unsure of, always taking the sure, known route, staying with something you've done repetitively for years—such "safe" approaches to life lead to neither joy or progress. And the real joy in life lies not in months or years or accumulated security, but in moments—moments when we take risks and allow ourselves to feel.

The same instructor also teaches skiing. You can guess what he says to his pupils on the hill. "Don't be afraid to fall down. When you fall down, it's proof that you're trying to go beyond what you could do before. If you're not falling down, you're not learning."

Richard:

We were at a California beach not long ago, early one morning, watching joggers and beach walkers. To avoid the waves and keep their feet dry, some walked high up on the beach, slogging through the loose, dry sand. Others risked the waves, running low and close to the breakers on the firm, smooth, wet sand. In life, the firmest, fastest footing where the greatest progress is possible is near the waves of risk.

Risk in this sense is not a synonym for foolishness or casual disregard for experience. Risk is valuing progress and uniqueness more than you fear failure or ridicule. Theodore Roosevelt said it this way: "In the battle of life, it is not the critic who counts. . . . The credit belongs to the man who is actually in the arena . . . who, if he succeeds, knows the triumph of high achievement; and if he fails, at least fails while daring (risking) greatly, so that his place will never be among those cold and timid souls who never knew either victory or defeat."

We have a friend, a former university professor, who seems to be concerned, more than anything else, about what he calls "too high a comfort level." He likes the quote "There is no progress in passing from ease to ease." Some time ago, he began to feel that his tenured position, his teaching of the same classes year after year, the respect and acceptance he enjoyed among students and other faculty—that all these were "dulling" him, raising his comfort level much too high. So he quit. He left the university and started other pursuits. Each of these pursuits was new, each was less secure, but each involved the risk that he feels makes him more alive.

Many botanists tell us that seeds, just before they burst into growth, begin to vibrate rapidly. People, before they begin to grow, begin the shaky process of taking risk.

Richard:

I have a close friend whom I have known since grade school. Although our lives have taken us in different directions, we still try to get together, once each summer, for a long walk and talk in a mountaintop forest near our childhood home. The talks are always candid. We give each other a type of feedback that would be impossible between people who didn't know each other well or who had known each other for less time.

One year he said something to me that I'm not sure he intended totally as a compliment. I took it as one, though, because it dealt with something about which I felt so strongly, particularly since I had been thinking about and working on *Lifebalance.* "You have always been," he said, "interested in doing different things, and in doing them in a different way. You want to do things differently than others do them—and differently than the way you have ever done them before."

Someone said, "Think of life as a struggle not to be influenced." Part of taking risk is daring to do different things in a different way. It is saying, "I know that is the ordinary thing to do, but why be ordinary?" It is saying, "I know that is the usual way of doing it, but I'm not sure it is the best way," or "I'm not so sure there is one 'best way.' "

This kind of thinking always involves the risk of criticism or jealousy. But you can comfort (and compliment) yourself with Einstein's quote: "Great spirits have always encountered violent opposition from mediocre minds."

Risk is related to feeling. Those who learn to relish rather than fear a certain amount of risk are more alive and feel more than those who avoid risk. Taking risks is one of the ways we can teach ourselves to feel.

E. E. Cummings said: "A poet is someone who feels and puts these feelings into words. Most people think or believe or know that they can feel but that is thinking, or believing, or knowing—not feeling. Anyone can be taught to think or believe or know, but not a single human being can be taught to feel."

It is a beautifully expressed statement. But it is *wrong*. People can be taught to feel. If not by others, they can teach themselves. One way to learn to feel is to take risks. Another way (an ironic one in light of what Cummings said) is to try to write poetry—to try to probe our hearts, first asking ourselves what we feel and then trying to express it.

Depth of feeling is in direct proportion to effort extended. Exerting ourselves physically causes us to feel tired but also strengthens our endurance. Mental effort allows us to feel both the fatigue and the exhilaration of observation and learning. Extending ourselves emotionally leads to deeper feelings and greater capacities to care and to love.

Now let's talk about a particular type of feelings and a particular kind of risk. We call these feelings impressions, hunches, intuition, or nudges, and following them always involves a certain amount of risk. Think for a moment about what *you* do with these feelings when they come. Too many people too often ignore them.

In a world oriented to hard data, information systems,

logic, and objective proof, there seems little place for something as subjective as a feeling or a hunch. In fact, we often put such things in the same category as superstition, horoscopes, or fortune-telling. We are modern, scientific people, and any data not received objectively through one of our five senses is suspect.

And it's too bad. Because carefully tuned intuitive feelings are often *more* reliable than sight, hearing, touch, taste, or smell. And the "nonprocess" of intuition can be at least as useful as the process of logic.

It's also too bad because ignored feelings gradually grow dim and disappear. When we stop trusting our feelings, we also stop valuing them. We stop welcoming feelings and we stop cultivating them. And pretty soon, they stop coming.

People who stop feeling in a sense stop living.

Feelings resemble radio signals in that they become stronger when they are carefully tuned in. The way to tune in on feelings is to notice them, appreciate them, probe and try to feel their full depth, and then act on them.

Some feelings, we strongly believe, resemble radio signals in another way. They come from an external source. The sureness feelings that tell us some things are right and other things are wrong; the flashes of insight feelings that we know are correct but can't trace by logic or cause and effect; the feelings of beyond-self strength that sometimes come when we meet an obstacle bigger than we can handle—these feelings come into us from without . . . from some intelligence far greater than our own. And the source is responsive to our requests.

Richard:

We have a friend in England, a remarkably accomplished and thoughtful man who is a member of Parliament and an acclaimed educator. He believes in (and attributes his own best thoughts and strengths to) a "highly superior intelligence" who has set up some sort of "access circuitry" into which we can "plug in" by asking and by listening in our minds.

Scott Peck, on the other hand, in his runaway bestseller, *The Road Less Traveled*, expresses belief in "a personal, loving God whose objective it is to help us become as He is."

We have been struck with the fact that irrespective of whether a person's beliefs resemble Peck's or the Parliament member's, it is completely logical to believe that the greater intelligence is both willing and able to assist our lesser intelligence.

Human beings are equipped with great capacity for intuition and feelings, and with the ability, when they look deep inside themselves, to know which of these feelings come from (or are confirmed by) a greater and wiser source.

Make friends with your feelings. Welcome them and nurture them. Take the time (and the risk) to let them deeper inside and to follow where they lead. Learn to ask yourself frequently not only how you feel but what you feel. Become good at asking the question—and good at answering it.

REVIEW: IMPLEMENTING ATTITUDE BALANCE ("JUMPING THE LINE" AND "RIGHT BRAIN RETENTION")

Okay, let's say you agree that you want to "get there" and "enjoy the journey," that you want to "act" and "respond;" that you want to develop and use the right hemisphere of your brain as well as the left, that you truly want to ride in jet planes and hot-air balloons, to be both structured and spontaneous, both disciplined and flexible.

Is "wanting" this kind of balance enough?

Nope!

Not nearly enough. We all want the balance; we all want both sides.

What most of us need is a fresh way of thinking—a new mental habit or two that trains our minds to go in both directions.

In other words, it's one thing to understand what you want and another thing to do it. It's one thing to know the type of person you want to be and another thing to be that type of person. It's one thing to believe or accept the ideas and principles in the section you've just read on attitude balance, and it's another thing to implement them.

But there is a habit that can change the way we see

and the way we do things, and that can make us into more disciplined and effective goal strivers at the same time as we are becoming more sensitive, more spontaneous, and more flexible.

The habit involves two things: (1) something called "serendipity lines" and (2) a new definition of a perfect day.

A serendipity line is simply a line from top to bottom, dividing a daily planning page in half. The day's schedule (which of course includes the *family*, *work*, and *self* priorities from the top of the page) is written on the left of the line—in an effort to "free the mind" from those lists and details as discussed in chapter 13.

The right-hand side of the page is left blank as a simple acknowledgment of the fact that many things will occur during the day that were *not* planned. There will be unanticipated needs, unforeseen opportunities, unexpected moments of beauty. There will be things to be responded to and to be enjoyed. In sum, if we develop the awareness described in chapter 15, and "slow down" as admonished in chapter 16, we will begin to discover serendipity.

Remember Walpole's original definition of serendipity from chapter 14. He intimated that while everyone is exposed to unexpected opportunities, needs, and beauties, the only ones who notice and recognize them are those who (1) are purposefully pursuing something—usually something else—and (2) are sagacious (sensitive and observant) enough to notice.

If you have goals and a plan for the day, then when you notice a possibility you had not planned, you are in a position to *choose* whether to stay with what you had planned or to "jump the line" and do the serendipity thing instead.

So the habit we are suggesting simply involves one little addition to the daily planning and working the triangle already presented in the last section. The addition is drawing a vertical serendipity line down the center of the page. Plan and schedule on the left and let the blank right side remind you to be playful, (chapter 17), to take risks, (chapter 20) and to be serendipitous. When you notice something better (or more needed) than what you had thought you would do, you "jump the line," deciding to spend time on it instead of on what you had planned to do. Write in these choices on the right side of your page and cross off the thing on the left that it replaced. (Note: The things on the left side will be written in future tense since they are plans and schedules. The entries on the right side will usually be past tense since you responded to them as they came up and made note of them after the fact.)

To make the habit work, you may need a new definition of a perfect day. Get rid of the idea that a perfect day is one in which you check off or cross off every single thing you had planned to do. (Let's call that a boring, robotlike day.) Instead, define a perfect day as one in which you accomplished most of the important things on the left of your line and also jumped the line two or three times to do serendipity things. With this kind of flexibility, you will be practicing antiplanning talked about in chapter 12.

Things that happen on the right-hand side are usually the most important things of the day. They usually fall into one of five categories: *needs*, *opportunities*, *people*, *ideas*, or *beauties*. They may be small needs, small beauties, small ideas. But the fact that they are small doesn't mean they are unimportant.

There is a second habit, a weekly or monthly one, that can enhance your ability to jump the line and that can help you keep track of the happy surprises and serendipity that have entered your life. It is called right brain retention, and it assists in the effort to live in the future, the present, and the past (chapter 19).

Occasionally, during your half-hour saw-sharpening on Sunday, go back through your daily plans and extract or index the things from the right-hand side that you want to retain or keep track of. (While you're at it, index the important things from the left side of the line, too.)

The easiest way to do this is to keep your daily planners and make a simple index of the needs, opportunities, people, ideas, or beauties (N,O,P,I, or B) that you have noted on the right side. The index for each month would probably consume less than a page and might start like this:

B June 2—exceptional sunset
P June 3—met Jeff Kramer
N June 3—played catch with Billy—talked about school problem
O June 4—saw special sale on lawnmowers
I June 5—ideas for disciplining teenagers from Pat
N June 6—helped Harry understand inventory system

From this index, you can locate and review the notes you made on the right-hand side of a particular day.

Taking fifteen minutes—perhaps on the first Sunday of each month—to perform the right brain retention and to "inventory" your serendipity for the month just past is a great habit to get into. It will not only help you retain and use the surprises and opportunities that have come along, it will make you more aware and appreciative of the value of the unplanned things in life. You will very likely realize that the things on the right side are as important if not more valuable and important than the planned things on the left-hand side. Thus the inventory will strengthen your commitment to serendipity.

C. GOAL BALANCE (BALANCING ACHIEVEMENTS WITH RELATIONSHIPS)

The third type of balance is *goal balance.*

Goals or objectives are generally thought of in association with accomplishments—with doing and with getting.

But goals can also have to do with relationships, and with becoming and giving.

It is not necessary to choose between people and things—but to avoid the choice, we must develop the ability to balance.

21. PEOPLE AND THINGS

Linda:

One busy weekend as I prepared a big Sunday meal, my four-year-old helper, Noah, who was sitting on our kitchen bar, inadvertently kicked a china bowl onto the floor. Richard had hand-carried that particular fine bone china bowl all the way from England, and he became uncharacteristically angry when he saw the smashed remains.

"Go straight to your room, Noah, and think about why it was that you knocked that bowl off with your foot," he demanded. "You know better than to sit on the bar!"

Obediently Noah left, weeping and wailing. Five minutes later he came back and looked up into his daddy's face. "What's more important," he said indignantly, "the bowl or me?"

What matters?

It's a question that runs through our minds fairly often in one form or another. But we don't usually think about it long enough or hard enough to answer it. And when we do answer the question, we find it hard to actively remember our answer long enough and consistently enough to implement it.

What matters is *people!*

People are usually less predictable than things. They are harder to manage, more exasperating, and they can hurt us more, or threaten us, disappoint us, or embarrass us. And people, if they are strangers with whom we have no connection, are much easier to leave alone than to get involved with.

But people are what counts.

Achievements are hollow and mean little unless they help people and are *for* people. As the old adage says:

> "Why build these castles glorious if man unheralded goes? Nothing is worth the building unless the builder also grows."

Richard:

A friend once told us that for the first time in years he had a little extra money and some vacation time coming. He was trying to decide between the two alternatives of adding a second bathroom to his modest home or taking his wife and three children on a family vacation. "We haven't been away together for years," he said, "but five people in one bathroom is ridiculous. I guess I'd better be practical, hadn't I?"

He sounded like he was trying to convince himself. We just listened and didn't offer much advice. We didn't see him for over a month, but when we did, he was beaming. "I did the practical thing," he said. We assumed he'd built the bathroom. But he went on, "We had the greatest trip.

It's something we'll never forget. What memories we made! I've decided that the most practical things are the things that last the longest, and these memories will last forever!"

We lived for three years in England. In the first days and weeks after the move, it seemed so delightful to have a new form of privacy. Since we didn't know anyone socially, we had long, uninterrupted evenings at home. It was great for a while. But we remember one night when we felt so uninvolved and so bored that we decided to simply go out and meet the neighbors. The evening was remarkable. We felt the exhilaration of meeting new personalities, challenging ourselves to relate to them, getting interested in their interests.

We took the children along. On the way home, our always enthusiastic eight-year-old said, "Wow, we must have the most interesting neighbors in the world. I think meeting new people is the funnest thing there is." The six-year-old picked up in his own way on the idea. "I think we should always talk to people, even if they're weird."

There is a unique kind of excitement in a new relationship. There are security and insight in old relationships. There is mutual benefit in friendly greetings or pleasant comments, even among strangers. Make the effort to say hello, to smile, to ask a thoughtful question, to pay a timely compliment, to start a conversation, and to keep in mind, constantly, the fact that people are more important than things.

22. "R GOALS" AND "L GOALS"

Goals. Objectives.

Some people love the words because they conjure visions of fulfillment, power, and control. Others are made to feel tired and discouraged by their mere mention.

Whether they pick us up or puncture us, the words usually bring to mind lists of things to do, left brain analyzing, logical planning, lightning-shaped check marks as action is taken.

"L goals," we could call them. Left-brain logic and lightning action applied to lists of accomplishment. L goals are quantitative and measurable and can be built like Lego blocks into stepping-stone, staircase sequences where short-term goals lead to long-term objectives.

"Get 'A' grade point average so I can get into 'X' university so I can get 'Y' job and make 'Z' money."

L goals lend themselves to achievement—or to failure—and make either one more obvious (at least to the goal setter). They do help people get further, faster and fancier—and most complaints against them are born of laziness or personal frustration.

As long as they are our tools and our servants, L goals are pluses. But when we give our devotion to them . . . to the extent that they become our masters, they begin to suck away our spontaneity, to force us away from flexibility, and to regulate us into the rigidity of robots.

But there is an antidote. It is called "R goals." Like an L goal, an R goal involves a vision of something as we want it to be. But R goals are as different from L goals as paintings are from mathematical equations.

R goals are usually oriented to relationships rather than achievements, people rather than things. They involve right brain ideas, intuition, and flashes of insight. They require responding and reacting rather than controlling and manipulating.

R goals are set by imagining a relationship the way you want it to be at some specific future point in time. R goals become more real if they're written (a description of a future relationship—with spouse, with a child, with a friend, with self).

An R goal is an image, complete with the feelings you want to attend the image. The image becomes reality not through careful planning or logical step-by-step implementation, but through the subconscious programming that the image causes in our own minds. Once this self-programming is in place, we automatically (and almost in spite of ourselves) begin doing the things, behaving in the manner, and thinking and saying the words that cause our present relationships to take on the imagined qualities of the image in our mind.

L goals are softened and controlled and kept in perspective by R goals, and R goals work best for a person who has the structure and discipline of L goals. In short, balance requires both.

Richard:

One Sunday night, early in our marriage, I sat down in our little apartment in Cambridge, Massachusetts, to review my goals. I had begun the practice of Sunday Sessions and had become a strong believer in the power of clearly set and vividly imagined goals.

That evening I reviewed my financial goals. I reviewed my career goals. I reviewed the goals I had for buying our first home, for getting in better shape, for learning to play the cello. I reread my calculation of what I wanted to have (and what I wanted to have done) in five years, then I went over what I had to do this year to be on course and in sync with the longer-range goals.

It was dusk on a lovely autumn day. I looked up from my papers and planners and gazed out on the sun's last light, reflecting on the Charles River. My mind drifted and daydreamed, and I found myself thinking that the most important things in my life were not the ambitions and objectives written on the pages in front of me. The important things were my wife, our new baby, my friends, my brothers and sister. The most valuable things in my life were relationships.

So why didn't any of my goals relate directly to the improving and perfecting of these relationships?

It was, I mused, because relationships couldn't

be quantified or measured. One couldn't very well say, "I have a ten-year goal of a perfect relationship with my wife . . . so my five-year goal is to have a 50 percent perfect relationship with her." No, relationships, by their very nature, did not lend themselves to goals or objectives.

But the sunset got even more beautiful and I kept gazing and kept thinking. The mind, when it could envision something, would lead you to it. If you wanted A's on your next semester's transcript, you had to write down the goal—conceive it and believe it—and then your mind would tell you, sometimes consciously and sometimes subconsciously, what you had to do to achieve it. Essentially, goals were clear mental images of things as you wanted them to become. So why couldn't they work with relationships?

Because relationships are harder to imagine and to describe than things or achievements. It's easier to "see" A's on a future report card or a certain amount of money in the bank by a certain date than it is to imagine something as complex as a relationship in the form that you would like it to be at some future time.

Yes, it is harder, I agreed with myself, but it isn't impossible, and relationships are worth whatever effort they require.

I ended up sitting in that same chair most of the night. I wrote a description of the relationship

I wanted to have with Linda five years from that date. I described the trust we would have between us, the confidence we would feel in each other, and the things we would each do for the other. The description also prompted me to write a list called "Linda is . . ." which reviewed what I knew about her makeup and her nature, and another list called "Linda needs from me . . ." which grew naturally out of the pondering my mind was doing.

Silver moonlight had now replaced the sun on the Charles, but once I was started, I couldn't stop. I wrote a description of the relationship I hoped I would have with my baby daughter by the time she was six years old. I enjoyed the imagination involved in thinking what she might be like, and trying to project the kind of father I wanted to be to her and the way in which I hoped she would think of me.

I decided the "relationship goals" would become a part of my Sunday Sessions—that I would take a few minutes each week to review my written descriptions and to think about my progress toward them.

Balance the L goals of your life with some R goals. Setting them will tax your imagination and test your writing ability, but the process will give you a hopeful, almost magnetic vision of the future and will refresh your perspective of what really matters in life.

23. GIVING THINGS UP MENTALLY

Now that we've talked about recognizing relationships as more important than achievements, and people as more important than things—now that we've done that, let's ask ourselves if it really has to be a choice. Is it either-or? Must we choose to be thing-oriented or people-oriented? Are achievers necessarily insensitive to relationships? Does the accumulation of things cause us to care more about things than about people?

These are tricky questions. A rather strong case can be made for the answer *yes*. Yes, it is a choice. Yes, financial or career achievements get in the way of relationships. Things often supercede people. There are some strong Scriptures and some solid spokesmen to back up this view. Thoreau felt that the antithing simplicity of a Walden Pond was necessary to maximize his relationships with God and self. Gandhi gave up all worldly possessions but his eyeglasses and Scriptures. The New Testament tells us that "a double minded man is unstable in all his ways" . . . that men cannot serve both God and mammon. Contemporary writers like Dwayne Elgren *(Voluntary Simplicity)* tell us that we should give up fancy food and modern convenience in sympathy for those in the world who have neither. For centuries, people have entered monasteries and deprived themselves of all but the most basic necessities and of any worldly recognition in order that they might reach deep into themselves and see into the hearts of others.

But there is another view. It is the view that sees both things and achievements as the means to ends that involve people and relationships. It is the notion that says, "Yes, I could give up plumbing in order to be more basic and humble and to better appreciate the plight of the poor, but then I would have to spend a lot of time pumping and carrying water—and I may be able to do something more useful for myself and for others with that time.

It is possible to accept the Bible's admonition and the examples and teachings of the Thoreaus and Gandhis of the world and to follow them mentally in our attitudes and priorities and perceptions—without throwing away everything that we have and living on the exposed side of a mountain. It is possible to change ourselves radically on the inside without starting over on the outside.

People who give up all possessions do so as a means of changing themselves inside. The process can work in reverse. As we impress ourselves with the truth that things don't matter, that achievements are of no real value unless they help people—once we see that clearly enough to change how we think—external changes in how we live are sure to follow.

Richard:

A friend who was staying with us received two bits of very bad news in the same day. The first was a phone call from his broker telling him that a major investment had experienced major losses. The second message also came by phone, this time from the person who was house-sitting his home, letting him know that his new, still uninsured car had been stolen.

He was a little shaken, but not much. I remember his words almost verbatim. "They're just things. They can be replaced. Except for your family and your health, you really can't lose anything very important."

An attitude like that leads to several benefits. First, it eliminates an incredible amount of worry. Second, it simplifies life by keeping us from having or even wanting a lot of material things that we don't need. Third, surprisingly, it helps us enjoy the things we do have more than we otherwise would.

Think about that third point for a moment. At first thought, it would seem that the more we care about a thing, the more we would enjoy it. If something is very dear to us—if we worry about it and hoard it and try to protect it and keep it safe—then we will get more pleasure from it, right? The more we value it, the more we enjoy it, correct? No! It works that way with people, but not with things. Those who overvalue things are so busy protecting them and worrying about them that they rarely enjoy them. On the other hand, those who see them only as things—things to be used, things to be appreciated, but things that could be replaced—truly enjoy the things they have.

Linda:

We get lots of practice giving up things mentally at our house. With the number of children and their friends who are running in and out of our house, the chances are about 60 percent that new things, nice things, and expensive things as well as sentimental things and invaluable things (hardly ever the worthless things) will be bashed, scratched, broken, bent, crushed, or wrecked within a short time.

The moving men drop our Steinway grand piano, the dogs ruin the new landscaping—even the deer eat the pine trees in the winter. Spending a long time worrying about these kinds of accidents could drive one crazy in a very short time.

The Scripture and wise philosophy of the world do not tell us not to have things; they tell us not to *value* things. The admonitions are mental, not physical. We should not treasure the things of the earth that moth and rust can destroy and thieves can steal. We should not trade time for things. If someone asks for our coat, we should give him our cloak also. This is not to say we should not take good care of our things, but it is to say that we should not be preoccupied with possessions.

One way to deal with the concept of possession is to eliminate it, to adopt the belief that we can't really possess or own anything anyway. The earth and all the things in it belong to God. We may have use or stewardship of things, but sooner or later they pass on to others. We should want the use only of what we can take care of and enjoy.

Many make the easy error of mistaking wealth or imagined possession with security. "I'm secure," they say, "because I've put lots away for a rainy day, because I have things." Real security is just the opposite. It is to be able to say, "I'm secure because I don't need any of those things. I could live without them. I am independent of them. If I lost them, I could replace them if I chose to." Security doesn't lie in the external score but in the internal abilities. A tennis player can be ahead but still very much afraid that he will lose. Another player may be behind, but quite secure in his knowledge that he has the ability to win.

The attitudes we are speaking of here are not easily or quickly adopted, but with conscious effort they can be obtained. Practice at not valuing things. Impress the attitude on yourself by repetition. Look for chances to demonstrate to yourself that things are tools to be used and enjoyed. Remind yourself that you're more interested in the things you need than in the ones you want; that you will quickly give up or give away a thing in favor of a person; and that it is *you* (rather than the world around you) who determines what you will value.

The rewards of your practice will be generosity, security, increased enjoyment, and a new perspective on almost everything.

24. BOTH!

People are more important than things, and relationships than achievements. When they conflict, the latter has to be given up (either physically or mentally) for the former. But we should reiterate that it usually doesn't have to be a choice. *Balance* has more to do with the words *both* and *blending* than it does with the words *either-or.*

Planning is often thought of as a science. And science, by definition, generally categorizes or separates things, divides apart and makes us choose between. One reason we call lifebalance "antiplanning" is that it is more an art than a science. Art tends to deal with combining things rather than separating them.

One of the central challenges (and opportunities) of lifebalance is mastering the art of consciously combining relationships with achievements—of blending people with things.

Richard:

It had been a horrendous month. I'd had to travel much more than usual, and time with the children had been almost nonexistent. Then still another unexpected (but "absolutely necessary") trip came up. After I stopped resenting the necessity and looking for a way out, I started looking for a way *in*, or a way to combine. It was a trip to Arizona which involved one meeting and one television appearance. If I spent some extra money, I realized I could take two of my daughters along.

It was a Friday and Saturday trip, so they would have to miss only one day of school.

It turned out to be a great experience. Alone with my two eldest children, away from the distractions and obligations of home, we talked more in two days than we had in two months. One daughter, fascinated with media and production, had the time of her life at the studio, where the producer let her sit in the control booth. The other girl, interested in art and architecture, was fascinated by the style and decor of the interesting hotel where we stayed.

Instead of coming home feeling behind on my relationships, as I usually do, I felt way ahead.

It's not only big trips where we can take children along, and it's not only major, planned situations where we can think of and integrate our relationships with our work. Take a child shopping or on an errand. Get to know the person you're buying from or selling to and make a friend as well as a deal. Bring your spouse to the luncheon meeting or on a service call. Notice a fellow employee's personality, skills, and interests as well as the fact that he's competing with you for the same promotion.

People are naturally inclined toward setting up false alternatives in their minds—toward thinking in terms of either-or—toward choosing one thing at the expense of another. So often, with a little thought, both are possible. Separate options can work together, and even assist and enhance each other. Often, in the long run, life is more a question of "both or neither" than of "one or the other."

This "all or nothing"/"both or neither" principle is a particularly appropriate way of thinking about achievements and relationships. We can't be completely people-oriented or totally thing-oriented because true accomplishments always involve relationships, and the best relationships often grow out of worthwhile achievements.

Look for ways to integrate family, friends, and relationships into the achievements of your life. Think of the tasks and pursuits of the day not only as checkoffs on your list or stair steps to your goals—think of them as ways to make new acquaintances, as opportunities to work with others, and as chances to involve or learn from or serve people.

25. NOURISHING FRIENDSHIPS

Some people collect rocks or stamps or coins. Others have learned to collect relationships and to cherish certain friendships that appreciate and grow in value more magically than the rarest collectible.

Almost everyone has heard (and repeated) the Will Rogers quote: "I never met a man I didn't like." Something inside tells us that there is good in everyone—that there is something we can learn from everyone. "But there's not time," we say—"We don't even have time for the friends we already have." Yet collecting relationships doesn't take much extra time, it just takes a different attitude toward the people we meet every day.

Learning to view "incidental" people as interesting human beings and potential friends rather than as part of the scenery takes some real concentration. But there is at least one very practical and one rather emotional reason for doing so:

1. People need people. A person you meet casually today may have a background, an ability, a capacity that you will need tomorrow. If you get to know a little about him, and if you remember him, he can become a *resource* that you may someday need. (The reverse is also true—he may need you and give you opportunities to serve or help.)

2. It is people—always people—who make life exciting. We are almost constantly surrounded by intrigue, by vast variety of experience, by diverse knowledge and insights of all kinds—in the form of the people around us. None of it flows to us without effort, but all of it is available to us if we learn to draw it out of the people who contain it.

Linda:

One summer while we were vacationing at a place called Bear Lake, in Idaho, we had an automobile accident. We hit a soft shoulder and bounced off a dirt road and through a fence into a boggy pasture. The bumps and bruises and the cast on a broken ankle kept us recuperating (and kept us grateful nothing more serious had happened) for a few days.

When things settled down, I remembered the fence and realized that I ought to pay to have it repaired. We didn't have much of our vacation left, and I was a little irritated that I had to spend time worrying about replacing barbed wire. So I drove back to the scene of the accident—in a hurry—planning to take care of this detail as quickly as possible.

It was a beautiful, golden day—the first hint of autumn in the air—and as I drove, my mood mellowed. By the time I got there I was over my hurry and remembered my goal of noticing people and collecting relationships. During the next hour I made friends with an interesting farm family, learned some fascinating things about the history of the lake, got some ideas about improving our own beach property, got my son (who had come along) involved in the friend-making conversation, and just generally had a great time—and, oh, incidentally . . . paid a small amount to cover some new barbed wire.

We so often think of people simply as objects who are part of (or sometimes barriers to) the things we want to get done. We need to reverse that and think of things and of tasks as situations that will bring us into contact with people—people whom we can get interested in, learn from, identify with, and enjoy.

Start collectiong relationships. In the same planner you use for daily planning, write down the people you meet each day—and what you learned about them, and what you learned from them, and what you liked about them. Review your notes at the end of the week in order to implant the new relationships into your memory. Take pride in moving toward a time when you have people you know and remember everywhere you go—relationships you have collected, friends you have made.

Linda:

We have moved about eight times since we got married. Each time after the kids are settled in schools and with friends, I feel a longing for interaction with nourishing friends of my own.

Although Richard is my best friend, I always need an "other mother" friend who will know what I mean when I say, "Eli and his little buddy played 'Singing in the Rain' with twenty pounds of unpopped popcorn in the storage room today."

In each new location I try to quickly organize what I call a "Mothers' Group," which consists of four or five women whom I think of as "soul sisters" and with whom trivia is cut to a minimum so that we can talk about ideas, books, stimulating people, and our own problems. We meet once a month and usually have a topic or a book to discuss.

As time has passed, women from the early groups have moved far from each other. Yet to this day, because of the things we shared, any of us can pick up the phone and start where we left off—truly nourishing each other with our friendship.

26. SELF-PROGRAMMING, SOLITUDE, AND RELATIONSHIP WITH SELF

You can jog your brain while you're jogging your body—and it will make them both respond better.

An incident that occurred several years ago led to the idea of the "self-programming" method for improving the relationship with self.

I passed George one day while I was jogging. He was running in the other direction. I said, "Hi," but he didn't seem to hear me. It looked as if he was talking to himself. His lips were moving. The second time around the block, we met again. He *was* talking to himself.

"Helloooo, George," I said—loudly.

His eyes glanced up as we passed. "Morning," he said, still hardly seeing me.

The third time I stopped him. "George, what are you

doing, building bridges while you run?" (George was a structural engineer.)

George looked at me, up out of the corners of his eyes (George was five feet four inches.) He was trying to decide whether to answer me. After squinting up at me for a moment, he said, "Run the other way around the block with me and I'll explain."

George liked to answer questions with questions. He said, "Why do you run?"

I said, "To stay in shape, to live longer, to enjoy the fresh air."

He said, "Mmmmmm, me too, but those are all secondary reasons for me. I jog to program my subconscious mind."

"To do what, George?"

"To self-program. What's happening while I jog is that I'm becoming a better person. I'm improving the way I relate to other people, and I'm making myself mentally stronger and more spontaneous."

George continued, between breaths as we jogged together: "Most people spend all their time trying to change things outside of themselves. They are working for a new car, a new TV. They are trying to change their jobs, to raise their salaries. They are trying to change their wives or their children. Often they are well-meaning. They want to change something for the better.

George glanced over to see if I was listening. I was. He went on: "I think the thing we should be working on is ourselves. The thing we ought to be trying to change is us—the inside. The only real way to change other people or things is to change yourself. If you want to be a better father, you don't change your kids; you change yourself. If you want to do better at your job, you don't change your work; you change yourself. If you want to help the kids in the class you teach, you change yourself into a better teacher and a better example."

"That's very interesting, George, but what are you doing to change yourself while you are running?" George was excited now. He was huffing and puffing but his voice had the tone of a Columbus telling about his discovery of a new world.

"Doctors tell us—psychiatrists, too—that exercise not only opens up the heart and the circulation, it opens up the mind, clears the cobwebs, makes the brain more receptive to ideas, to what I call *self-programming.*"

"What do you mean by that, George?"

"Well, you see, the subconscious mind is programmed by the input it receives. When I fail at something, my subconscious gets a message that I can't do it. When I hook the golf ball with my driver, my subconscious gets the message that I can't hit straight. But when I succeed at something, my subconscious gets a positive bit of programming. We are all our own creators, in a way. What we do and think makes us what we are."

"Yes, but what about the running, George?"

"I'm getting to that. You see, the interesting thing about the subconscious is that it can't tell the difference between something that happens and something that is thought. And it can't tell the difference between something someone else says to it and something you say to it. So I pick things I'd like to be and I tell myself I already am! For example, while I'm running I say to myself: "I am a spontaneous person. I notice unexpected beauty and unplanned opportunities." Then I think about evidence of this: how I noticed the clouds between the mountains last week, the surprise I found for my wife at the auction. My subconscious believes it. I become more what I want myself to be."

I liked what George was saying, liked it enough that I began to try it myself. My own major priorities were my wife and my children. I decided I would quit trying so hard to change them and instead use George's method to change myself—as a husband and as a father.

It was an interesting process. I identified some areas that I felt I needed to improve on, then refined them into a small number of qualities that I wanted to obtain. For the first little while, as I jogged, I simply thought about each quality for a moment and tried to imagine the setting and circumstances in which I could apply it. As time went by, I was able to think of, while I ran, occasions when I had applied those qualities. Thus I was able to start saying to myself, "First word: confidence. I show confidence in my children. They feel my pride in them. I keep criticism and belittling out of my tone of voice and put confidence into my tone of voice. I look for chances to compliment them and to 'catch them doing something good.' Yesterday I told Saydi how creative her school projects are, and I saw her take on the confidence I felt in her."

I soon became aware that I was exhibiting some of the qualities subconsciously, without thinking about them. I found that I was more aware of the children and of the teaching moments that presented themselves. I was, by then, doing less planning of specific activities and time with the children but was actually spending more time with them. And it felt less of a burden. I seemed to react instinctively with the answer or example they needed.

Pick out a few key adjectives that describe the type of person you want to be, the type of parent you want to be, the type of spouse you want to be. Create your own complete definitions for your chosen words—making them mean the quality you desire.

Then pick out some routine task or activity that you do each and every day (driving to work, jogging, shaving, or putting on makeup in the bathroom, etc.) and use that time to think through your words—and to program them into who you are.

Linda:

Often the only privacy I have during the day is a few moments first thing in the morning in the bathroom. That is where I do my "self-programming."

While there, I also try to visualize my day. I don't have to wonder if there will be a tense situation or a crisis. I am absolutely sure there will be. Knowing that I'll be walking into a "hurricane," I resolve that I will be the "eye," or the calm center of the storm that swirls around me.

I can see myself responding kindly to a screaming two-year-old, reasoning logically with a stubborn ten-year-old boy, and ignoring outrageous statements by teenagers. Sometimes I even rehearse my lines: "Let's talk about it." "Things will look better in the morning." "I understand how you must feel!"

Although I say what I visualized I would say only about 40 percent of the time, the atmosphere in our home is usually much better than it was when I was always just "doing what comes naturally."

Self-programming is a way of creating yourself and of developing chosen characteristics within yourself.

The other inner thing we need to do, and something that is quite different, is to search for and accurately identify the things that are already inside us . . . to find and feel our truest nature, our deepest beliefs, our best ideas. Doing so requires solitude, and solitude, in today's world, is surprisingly hard to find. As an urban society, we are constantly around other people, and in the moments when we could be alone, we turn on the television and resurround ourselves.

To find solitude we sometimes have to go to the desert or the mountains or the sea. Or we have to get up early in the morning or stay up late into the night. But there is a rest and a rejuvination in solitude that makes it worth whatever effort it takes.

Self-programming and visualizing are ways to alter who we are. Perhaps an even deeper need is to discover who we are. Self-discovery occurs in solitude. It is easier to find ourselves when we are alone, and to find the best and clearest (and most unique) thought that is in us. It has been said that "genius is alone."

One who thinks alone will gain ideas that are new—or at least ideas that are his or her own. And whether or not the thoughts are unique, they will be original and fresh and very likely understood or expressed in a brand-new way.

The question is often asked: Why were there so many original thinkers, so many great men of ideas and clarity and philosophical courage just over two hundred years ago as this country was born? The population of the country was tiny, yet more great individuals seemed to emerge in that era than do today from our vastly larger population. Part of it may have been the challenge of the time, and much of it may have been the inspiration of God. But another part was the solitude these people had—the life-styles and the situations of those times which gave individuals the time and the opportunity to think on their own and to explore and extend their ideas in the privacy of their own minds.

Today, because of our urban life-style and our ever-present print and electronic media, we are surrounded and bombarded by the thinking of others—to the extent that any ideas we have feel a little secondhand, a little brainstormed or overcooked, a little *Osterized* by the mixing, sloshing education and communication systems around us.

A quiet mind, alone, uninterrupted, uninfluenced by outside clatter or the perspectives of others, is a fertile seedbed for new thought—and for thoughts that perhaps could grow nowhere else.

Get away. Find both a time and a place for solitude, and go there regularly if not often. Bring along a journal and a pen. Look inside yourself and inside your mind, and make some notes on what you find there.

The combination of self-programming and solitude can unlock the deepest parts of ourselves and energize our relationships with ourselves and with those around us.

27. RESERVED TIME

One way to avoid the neglect of important relationships is to make some standing appointments that never change.

Instead of giving our families (and ourselves) only our "leftover time"—only the bits of time that don't happen to be taken up by other things—we need to block out some "prime time" which is only for relationships. Think about the possibilities on the following list, and either adopt some of them or design some for yourself. What we've said so often applies again here—don't even try to do all these things—just pick one or two that you like.

1. *Tuck-in time.* Often the best time to communicate with smaller children (adolescents, too, for that matter) is as they are tucked into bed. It's a natural time to talk about the day just past—its problems, its feelings. Set aside a certain number of nights each week to do the tucking in.

2. *Dinner hour.* Traditionally, the dinner table has been the place of family communication. The day's events were discussed and shared. What was common "then" is uncommon now. Families rarely eat together. Fast foods and busy schedules have turned eating into a process of "refueling." Change it back! Set aside certain nights when

you will eat together as a family—spend a dinner hour and talk together.

3. *Both sides of bed.* The early morning is a magnificent time that most people either sleep through or hurry through. And the still, late hours that can be so thoughtful and reflective are too often spent passively in front of a TV. Learn to view the late and early moments as your time—your time to meditate, read, ponder, plan, pray—your time to improve your relationships with self and with God.

Richard:

Sometimes I come home a little late
and the house is quiet and still
and dark with shadows.
I take my shoes off and pad around quietly
from bedroom to bedroom,
Tucking in sleeping children, remarkably
    angelic
in their slumber.
I look in on each
like a miser, counting his wealth.

4. *Sundays.* The notion of the sabbatical—of one time period in every seven that is used for rethinking and as a change of pace—is a clear and valid concept. But Sundays

have become the day of the big game or the big party or the big outing. Change your definition of Sunday recreation—make it mean "re-creation." Set aside time to think, to reflect, to rest, and to work on relationships with your family and with your inner self.

5. *The weekly date.* If you're married, continue your courtship by reserving one night each week for a date.

6. *The five-facet review.* As discussed earlier, if you have a family, use your weekly date once a month as a time to go to a quiet restaurant and discuss your children. Conduct a five-facet review (chapter 8) of each child by asking yourselves: "How is Johnny doing physically? Mentally? Emotionally? Socially? Spiritually?" Take notes. Pick out one or two areas where you need to concentrate your parenting during the month ahead.

7. *Transition time.* The time when you come home from work and enter your home is the key transition of the day. Instead of bringing the cares and frustrations of work in with you, you want to leave them behind and focus on relationships—especially during the first few minutes after you arrive. Pause before you enter your home. Make the transition mentally. Decide in advance to walk in and be totally with your family.

8. *Family night.* Reserve one night a week to do something with your family. Regard it as almost sacred, and don't let anything allow you to ignore or forget it. Don't let yourself rationalize your way out or give up. It can be anything ranging from having ice cream together at home, to holding a family council, to teaching the children a lesson you want them to hear, to attending a basketball game or the ballet. It's time in the bank which creates wonderful memories.

9. *Morning devotional.* Get up early enough to spend ten or fifteen minutes together as a family before breakfast and before leaving for work or school. Read Scripture and hold family prayer if you have religious convictions. If not, spend a few moments reading together or memorizing whatever you deem to be motivational and insightful, and discuss plans and goals for the day.

Your time is yours. Before you give it away to the world, take some select little bits of it out—and set them aside. Reserve them for relationships.

28. MORALITY AND PRACTICALITY

A television correspondent who had recently completed an in-depth report on AIDS was asked for his personal, bottom-line conclusion. "This is a case," he said, "where traditional morality and simple practicality run exactly parallel."

Question: Does traditional morality *always* run parallel to practicality? Are the basic values that we call morality the most practical, safe, dependable and happy guidelines for how we should live?

Richard:

I have an acquaintance who is a highly trained, high-priced psychiatrist—and a very competent and caring person. A few years ago he was attending a church where the congregation's leader was a lay minister who was, by profession, a plumber.

Over the course of several months, the psychiatrist observed that several of his patients were members of the same church and were also going to the lay minister for guidance. Alarmingly, he also observed that these people seemed to be benefitting more from the plumber-minister's free advice than they were from his costly consultation.

He finally went to the minister and asked him to reveal the secret of his success in counseling and helping troubled people. The plumber answered easily and quickly. "Why, it's easy, really," he said, "I just talk with them until I find out which commandment they're breaking—and then I tell them to stop it!"

Christians and Jews may call their values "The Ten Commandments." Taoists may call theirs "The Way." Buddhists, Hindus, and members of Islam have their own names for very similar codes of conduct and values. Atheists and agnostics, while not ascribing the principles to a deity, nonetheless usually adopt philosophies that embrace similar rules of conduct and comparable basic values.

So, whether our source is religion or philosophy or just plain personal logic, the directions are similar if not identical. They are directions of honesty; of respect for life, property, family and the commitments of marriage; of unselfishness and caring for each other; of setting aside some time for worship, meditation or solitude; of avoiding greed and jealousy; and of self reliance, discipline and responsibility.

"Traditional morality" and "universal values" are interesting terms. They point out the fact that both logic and history teach us that certain ways of thinking and behaving work better than their alternatives.

The fact is that a moral lifestyle works better than any other lifestyle.

The fact is that traditional morality always runs parallel both to practicality and to happiness.

And many would go further and say that immoral or amoral lifestyles always lead to some form of unhappiness or some kind of sickness—either physical, mental, or emotional.

The irony is that we live in a country with Judeo-Christian origin and orientation where seven out of the ten biblical "commandments" are broken routinely—usually without guilt and without thought. We are better at professing morality and traditional values than we are at living them.

We live in a society where people are looking for happiness in all the wrong places—and not finding it.

But, thank God, we also live in a society where we are free to choose our own lifestyle, our own priorities, our own morality.

And, despite it's absence in most popular movies, music, and media, a substantial number of Americans still subscribe to "traditional morality" . . . and try to live a life of discipline and correct priorities.

The case that is usually made for traditional values and morality is often religious or "preachy" in its tone and wording. And the case against them is often based on arguments of freedom and individual choice. Overlooked is the aspect of practicality and the common sense conclusion that we ought to be willing to learn from the collective experience of every generation of humanity that has preceded us.

Linda:

We have a minister friend who says he thinks the word "commandments" and its authoritarian connotations are unfortunate. So he uses a different wording. He calls the Biblical laws "The ten points of loving counsel from a wise father." What he means is that God, who to him is an infinitely wise and benevolent father, has given us freedom of choice on this earth so we can grow—but has also counseled us on how to be happy—given us advice on the type of behavior that leads to the happiest life.

Whether we are religious believers or not, ignoring the established values, morality and "commandments" of history and society is the moral equivalent of rediscovering the wheel.

When we try to be completely objective and practical about the whole thing, it may come down to something as basic as time—and the fact that we each have a limited amount of time in our lives.

During a lifetime we may have long enough to learn the truth and validity of a lot of principles for ourselves—by trial and error, but if we spend our lives learning lessons in this way, we will have time for little else, and we will suffer through more unhappiness and heartache than is necessary.

The meaning and validity of basic moral values are not vague or mysterious. The cause-and-effect aspects of them are rather obvious and straightforward. If we honor our parents, we create happiness both for them and for us. If we rest and renew ourselves on Sunday, we are better off for it. If we do not worship things other than God, and if we avoid jealousy and coveting it will help us steer clear of the selfishness and greed that guarantees unhappiness. If we respect other people's lives and property, we will also respect ourselves more, and others will return our respect. And if we honor our marriage vows, we will create a deeper, more fulfilling, and more lasting partnership with our spouse.

If there is an underlying guideline or objective for this book, it is to propose solutions that work and that create happiness. Nothing qualifies more as a solution; nothing has been proven to "work" more often; nothing has more consistently worked against unhappiness; and nothing gives a person more time to pursue his gifts and develop himself . . . than simple acceptance of and adherence to what we have come to call traditional moral values.

29. FEELINGS AND HONESTY

Unexpressed feelings never die, they just get buried and come forth later in uglier forms.

There are two fundamental keys in all deep and genuinely beneficial relationships. One is empathy and the other is honesty. Unfortunately, we sometimes operate under the confused notion that the two are not compatible. Empathy means being sensitive to the other person's feelings, while honesty has to do with being candid about our own feelings. If our own honestly expressed feelings are upsetting to the other person, we reason, then expressing them would not be empathetic.

It all depends on the type of relationship we are dealing with—and on the kind of relationship we want it to become. For the sake of simplification, let us categorize relationships into two groups: A. Important, deep, long-term relationships where the goals are trust, mutual sharing, useful feedback, and sometimes even oneness. B. Superfluous, surface relationships where the goals are "not to rock the boat" and to avoid friction, differences, or hurt feelings.

In a "B" relationship, the old adage "some things are better left unsaid" is a wise guideline. In an "A" relationship, it is a slow-acting but deadly poison pill. It may be true that some hurtful, critical comments are best left unsaid during a moment of anger, but real feelings cannot go unsaid too long before they begin to fester and grow uglier than they originally were.

Often we make the mistake of confusing the objectives of a B relationship with the objectives of an A relationship. The goal of an A relationship is not to avoid conflict. Rather, the goal is to grow individually and grow collectively by reasoning together, learning from each other, sometimes through debating and resolving conflict.

Linda:

When we were first married I assumed the best thing to do when I was upset or angry was to try to forgive Richard of his shortcomings and muffle my anger. Luckily he figured this out when I started slamming drawers. When asked what was wrong, I would icily retort, "Nothing!" After a short time he convinced me that he really wanted to know.

The first thing I remember telling him was that it drove me crazy that he had to eat a fourth meal every night in bed at eleven o'clock, particularly when he could make soft little raisins sound like celery. "It's especially annoying," I said, "when I'm on a diet and starving to death while you're chewing away on food that smells divine!"

He agreed to stick to as quiet and as nonaromatic food as possible.

As the years have passed, I have become so good at expressing my feelings that I think he regrets having ever taught me. Several times he has mentioned that he still likes me to tell him how I feel but that it would be great if I could do so a little more nicely!

Often hurt feelings and disagreement have brought about major wars, but they are short-lived—sometimes hours but rarely days. Therefore, the air is usually clear and our lives are generally much more productive.

Partners in a relationship need to develop enough trust so that they can accept and even welcome differences without worry or concern that the relationship is threatened. And they need to feel that they can honestly and candidly express their feelings, even when these feelings may be upsetting or unflattering to the other person, with full confidence that a meeting of minds can be reached.

Richard:

Early in our marriage, partly because we were still learning to communicate (as we still are) and partly because our work and schooling separated us so often, we had some problems with "unexpressed feelings that got buried and came forth later in uglier forms."

We had started, by that time, the process of having Sunday Sessions, a half hour individually to work on some plans for the coming week, followed by a meeting to work out our schedule together.

One week, when we were both aware of some "unexpressed feelings," we decided to add a little extra part to our meeting. We called it "How I feel and how I felt." I remember it clearly because Linda started by telling me she loved me—and respected me . . . needed me. She then told me of two times during the past week when she had been very upset at me but hadn't found a way or a time to tell me about it. In the context of our meeting and the feelings she had just expressed for me, I was able to accept the criticism implied by what she had felt earlier.

In turn, I shared a couple of things that had bothered me. It cleared the air. We both felt better. So we adopted the idea, decided never to let anything fester for more than a week, and began to hold a short "how I feel and how I felt" discussion as part of each Sunday Session.

Decide which of your relationships are "A" relationships. Within them, commit yourself to full disclosure of feelings. Do not share selectively, share totally. Find ways that work for you—ways of expressing and uncovering what you feel rather than burying it.

30. SEEING BEYOND EYESIGHT AND THE POWER OF QUESTIONS

The most important relationship of all is vertical rather than horizontal. And it involves gratitude, humility, wonder, and awe.

Theodore Roosevelt, affected occasionally by feelings of importance and indestructibility, often invited his friend, the eminent naturalist William Beebe, to be an overnight guest at the White House. Their habit was to walk out onto the west balcony at dusk and watch the oncoming night and the emergence of the stars. As they appeared, Beebe would name them and tell Roosevelt their size and how many light years they were away from the earth.

At a certain point he would say, "See that faint spot of light mist just beyond the lower left corner of the great square of Pegasus? It looks like a dim star, but it is actually the great spiral galaxy of Andromeda. It is as large as our Milky Way galaxy, which contains every star we can see. Andromeda is seven hundred fifty thousand light-years away and contains a hundred billion stars. And it is only one of hundreds of millions of galaxies. . . ."

At that point, Roosevelt would say, "I think we feel small enough now, William. Let's retire."

We are small. We live in a universe that is vast beyond our comprehension.

From the very beginnings of understanding, man has pondered this vastness, considered the overwhelming organization of it all, and generally taken it as an indication, if not a proof, of a greater intelligence, of a power infinitely beyond man's.

But if there is compelling evidence of deity, it lies less in the incomprehensible bigness of things than in the intimate smallness of what happens inside of us in quiet moments when we are alone but do not feel alone.

Irrespective of people's religion (or their lack of it), most have concluded (or realized) that there are sources of knowledge or of insight other than the five senses. Buddhists call our inner perceptions "the eye of truth," "the eye of the soul," or "the eye of the heart." Rumi, the great Persian poet, wrote of "the eye of the heart . . . of which these two sensible eyes are only the gleaners." St. Augustine said that "our whole business in this life is to restore to health the eye of the heart by which God may be seen."

From where does our "beyond-senses" insight come? Is it a product of our mind's ability to link together subconscious data and recall consciously forgotten information? Or does it come to us (or into us) from an external and higher intelligence and a greater power?

It is a personal question and requires a personal answer that only you can give. Regardless of how you answer it, the next question is how to tap in, how to get extrasensory insight into things like self, purpose, direction, and meaning.

That last question is an interesting one because the answer is a question. The way to get the answers is to ask the questions. Ask who you are. Ask where you came from. Ask why you are here. Ask what you should be doing with your life. Ask if there are better places for you than where you are now. Ask big questions and small questions. Ask questions even when you have no idea where to look for the answers. Ask them even if you are unclear about just who you are asking.

We live in an age that is oriented too much to answers and not enough to questions. A truly educated man is not one with all the answers but one who knows how to ask the right questions. Questions are not a sign of weakness or doubt. They are a sign of the deepest kind of security, and they are the trigger if not the source of all the information and insight we will ever get.

If you believe in God, direct your questions to Him, for it is only logical that: (1) He knows the answers, (2) He would like you to have at least some of them, and (3) He understands, whether you do or not, the means whereby He can give them to you.

If you don't believe, ask the questions of yourself. Chances of an answer exist only when the question has been asked.

Keep track of the insight questions you ask (to God or to yourself). Write them in a journal, jot them down during Sunday Sessions. Refer back to them often. Re-ask them often. Occasionally you will return to a question and find, to your delight and perhaps to your surprise, that it has become an answer.

REVIEW: IMPLEMENTING GOAL BALANCE ("RELATIONSHIP BANDS" AND "TWO-EDGED GOALS")

As with the other two forms of balance, the principle or theory of goal balance is easier to accept than it is to implement. We know that people are more important than things (chapter 21); that relationships are usually more lasting than achievements, that the two should be combined wherever possible (chapter 24), that we should nourish and develop friendships (chapter 25), that what happens in the inside of our homes and the inside of ourselves counts more than what happens on the outside.

It's easy to nod our heads and acknowledge all of this, but in the busy demands of the day-to-day, it's not easy to bring the balance about. What it takes, like the other two forms of balance, is a weekly habit and a daily habit.

We call the weekly habit "two-edge goals." Like a two-edged sword, two-edged goals cut both ways. They carve out achievement and accomplishment on one side; and they shape better relationships on the other side.

The habit is a simple one. During your weekly Sunday Session, spend equal time on L goals and R goals (chapter 22). List the things you want to accomplish during the week, then think about the key relationships of your life and how you want them to be. In your first few Sunday Sessions, write out some "future relationship descriptions." After they are written, simply spend a little time each Sunday reading them—reviewing them—perhaps adding a bit to them. As you review these descriptions or relationship goals each Sunday, they will feel more and more real and you will find the actual relationships of your life conforming to what you have described.

The daily part of the habit is equally simple. Use a highlighter or nonpenetrating felt-tip marker to make three horizontal "relationship bands" across your daily plan or schedule. Put one band across the very top, one across the very bottom, and one about two-thirds of the way down the page.

These relationship bands represent the "reserved time" discussed in chapter 27—time that is reserved for the important relationships of life. The top band is the early-morning time often used for strengthening our relationship with God and with self. It might be used for meditation, for Scripture or prayer, for seeking beyond-senses insight (chapter 30), for self-programming, talked about in chapter 26 or perhaps in the effort to prioritize and give things up mentally (chapter 23). The middle band is the dinner hour, or the transition time when you come home from work. For a woman whose career is her home, the transition would be the time when the children come home from school. It is time set aside to listen, to ask, to communicate, to find out all you can about what each other feels and thinks and needs. The last band, at the end of the day, might be for your marriage relationship—a time to talk, to plan the next day together, or to openly discuss feelings together, as mentioned in the preceding chapter. It might also be a time for important relationships with friends—to visit, to make a phone call, and so forth.

The important thing about relationship bands is that they are *reserved*. You quit thinking about things and quit worrying about what needs to be done during these brief interludes, and you focus on relationships and on the people who are closest to you. These reserved times can be flexible in length—perhaps a long one some evening as you tuck children in bed and tell stories, perhaps a short one another night when all there is time for is a long look in the eyes, a pat on the head, and a sincere "I love you." The important thing is that the relationship bands happen—every day.

D. WHAT DOES IT TAKE?

Take a stand!

That is what you must do if you want lifebalance.

If you want to swim your own course rather than being swept along by the world's currents, if you want to judge yourself by your own definition of success, if you want to make what you do match with what you believe, then you must take a personal stand.

Hopefully, *Lifebalance* will help you design and implement the stand you take.

Richard:

Please don't get the idea, from the personal illustrations in many chapters, that the Eyres have achieved total lifebalance. Naturally we've used our most positive experiences as examples. It doesn't mean we don't have negative experiences, and it doesn't mean we don't struggle!

We have made a strong commitment to the idea of lifebalance, and it has changed the way we think and the way we live. But we certainly haven't arrived.

The point is that you never do! Lifebalance is a journey, not a destination. It is a worthwhile, rewarding, ongoing struggle, and sometimes what we are struggling against is the world around us—the norms, the expected.

Before you decide to take a stand, you should know what the stand takes.

Three things!

1. A commitment to a new pattern of thinking where you ponder the three balance points and what you choose to do about each of them each day *before* you think about your schedule and what you have to do that day.

2. More awareness! And a willingness, even an anxiousness, to break your schedule and leave your list

when you notice something more important or more beautiful.

3. A few minutes every day to work the triangle and draw the serendipity line. And a half hour every Sunday (the saw sharpener) to think ahead through set two-edged goals and to think back through right brain retention.

E. A TRIANGULAR MODEL FOR BALANCE

The symbol of a corner-nesting triangle split by a vertical line represents the three types of balance that this book has discussed. Whether or not you use the lifebalance system that follows, the symbol will serve as a summary.

As mentioned earlier, a triangle is a figure or symbol of balance. It has no opposite corners, each line is connected to each other line, and like a tripod, it will balance and sit solidly on uneven ground.

The three priorities we all try to balance (family, work, and self) are the three corners or "balance points" of the triangle. View the diagram as three separate corners—pushed together so that they nest within each other.

The left corner represents work or career and is the

outer figure in the logo since it occurs outside the home, or at least is external to the family itself.

The right "family corner" nests mostly inside because it deals with things inside the home. And the "self" or "character" corner is deep within the symbol because it represents what is inside of us.

The three priorities or corners can be referred to as "the outer," "the inner," and "the inner-inner."

The vertical line drawn through the triangle represents balance between the structure and scheduling of the left hemisphere of the brain and the spontaneity and serendipity of the right brain. This is the balance between acting and responding, between getting there and enjoying the journey. And it is often the balance between achievements and relationships, between things and people.

Note how the different types of balance come together in the symbol. The reason that the left corner of the triangle falls to the left of the center line is that, in most cases, work is a left brain function and deals with achievement-type goals. However, part of this corner goes across to the right of the line because relationships and spontaneity should also be a part of work.

"Family" is represented by the right, "inner" corner of the triangle because families are mostly a question of relationships, responding to needs, and using the spontaneous, flexible right hemisphere of the brain. Part of the corner crosses to the left side, however, since families do need some structure and some achievement goals.

The top (and inner-inner) corner of the triangle symbolizes the self—the heart—the character that should be equally balanced between the structure, planning, and achievement of the left and the serendipity, flexibility, and relationships of the right.

It is important, if you choose to get into the lifebalance system that follows, to keep in mind the meaning of the symbol and the three types of balance it represents. Whatever level of planning and balance we are discussing (daybalance, monthbalance, yearbalance, etc.), we will be dealing with all three corners or balance points and with both the "structured left" and the "flexible right."

PART FOUR

SUMMARY (A NINE-STEP SYSTEM FOR GETTING YOURSELF BALANCED)

Balancing is a process that is best worked into through a sequential, nine-step system that can change the patterns of how we think. Each step is named after the concept it is built on.

The *Lifebalance* system is simply an organized, nine-step sequence for implementing the kind of balancing and antiplanning that this book has advocated.

Because the techniques involved in each of the nine steps have already been mentioned earlier in the book, this system provides a summary as it puts the steps together in the order that we think lends itself best to implementation. It also gives us a chance to take some of the concepts mentioned earlier and illustrate them.

SUMMARY

Please remember several things as you go into this system:

First, remember that *Lifebalance* comes intentionally with a little of its own terminology and jargon. Words like *serendipity line* or *balance points* not only make it easier to explain the system, they become part of our vocabulary and remind us and motivate us to stay with it and make it work. The *name* of each of the nine steps is one of the new *lifebalance* terms, and each step *begins* with a brief definition of its new term.

Second, remember that we call the system *antiplanning* because it is designed to pull in the opposite direction of most time management. It provides a basic grid of structure and goals, but it pulls toward flexibility and spontaneity, toward family, relationships, and inner growth.

Most planners or time management tools imply that the way to be successful is to do more things, be more efficient, waste less time, fill up every minute.

Lifebalance, on the other hand, agrees with the ancient Oriental saying, "To the noble art of getting things done we must add the more noble art of leaving things undone." Lifebalance attempts to increase not the quantity but the quality of the things we do.

Third, remember that bad habits of unbalance can be broken only by substituting good habits of balance. We said earlier that systems were part of the problem, but we were speaking of highly structured list-making systems that rob us of spontaneity and sensitivity. The unbalanced habits of bad systems can be broken with the balanced habits of a good system.

Lifebalance is not a detail-oriented, mind-occupying scheduling system. Rather, it is a priority-oriented, mind-freeing program of simplifying that helps people implement the three kinds of balance discussed in this book. Most of the steps in the program are just basic good habits.

Fourth, remember that the steps we are going to present are not the only way or the best way to implement balance. You may develop your own way. Please don't feel threatened by a step-by-step system—and don't feel restricted. Don't even feel compelled by it. You've already read the ideas and content of the book. This last section doesn't contain any additional philosophy—just a summary of what we've said already, in the form of a program for simplifying and practicing the concepts of lifebalance. Remember that we've already covered the principles. What's left to review is the procedures.

Conscientiously implemented, step one will bring about noticeable improvements in balance. Each successive step will enhance and add to that balance. The first four steps have to do with daily balance. The fifth step involves weekly balance, which can become a framework or guide for daily balance. The sixth and seventh steps develop monthly balance, which in turn makes the weekly balance more in tune and connected. Steps eight and nine deal with longer-range balanced goal setting, which provides "targets" at which we can aim our monthly and weekly balance.

STEP 1. BALANCE POINTS

The three areas of life (work, family, and self) that need daily attention if balance is to be obtained.

The first step is to decide and to commit. Decide to personally adopt the goal of balancing family with self with *work*. Commit yourself to making yourself do the hard mental effort that is required to bring about this balance.

The first step in changing our thought is to change what we think *about*. By adopting the conscious goal of building our lives solidly on all three balance points, we re-form our thought patterns and readjust where we spend our mental energy.

STEP 2. PRIORITY BLANKS

The three lines that are filled in each day *before* any scheduling is done—one line for each of the three balance points. The process of deciding on the single most worthwhile thing you can do each day for each balance point is called *working the triangle*. The few moments of thought required is called the *five-minute sit-there*, taken from the turned-around cliché, "Don't just do something, sit there."

Think of a day as a blank piece of paper.

The day is tomorrow. It's close, it's almost here, but it hasn't started yet. So it's blank, clean, undetermined. What do we want to write on our day?

What is important to us? What should we write on it for ourselves before we show it to the world—before we give it to others and let them start deciding where we will be, what we will do, who we will see, how we will spend our time?

Before you write anything, and before you think about what you have to do, or even about what you can accomplish, draw three little horizontal lines (priority blanks) at the top of your page and ask yourself what is the single most important or meaningful thing you could do that day in each of the three balance points of self, family, and work.

Many things may come to mind that you have to do in your job. And perhaps nothing specific comes instantly to mind for your family or for yourself. But think hard about all three areas for five minutes and decide what the main need is for yourself,* and for your family, and what one thing is most important at work. Then write these three priorities on your three priority blanks.

When you have finished, the top of your page might look something like this: (The little angles represent the three balance points or corners of the triangle as explained on page 226.)

∧ Do Aerobics

> Discuss "Boy Problem" with Lisa

< Get Jim's support on new idea

If you use a planner or time management tool, draw your three priority blanks in at the top of each day and

* Remember that the area of self includes service to others as well as personal development of self.

think about them *before* dealing with the details and commitments and schedule of the day. If you don't use a planner, put your priority blanks on a plain sheet of paper.

Try it for ten days. Some of the things you write on your priority blanks may be very small things ("Compliment Bill on yesterday," "Take solitude walk," "Call Wendy"), but they are things you consciously decided were important for one of your balance points. After ten days, their cumulative effect will become more evident to you—ten specific things you have done for family or a family member, ten specific things you have done for yourself, and no day in which you did not do something for each of the three balance points.

After ten days, you will have at least the beginnings of a new habit of balance, and you will be ready to go to step three.

STEP 3. RELATIONSHIP BANDS

Small segments of each day that are reserved for relationships; *transition times* during the day when one consciously focuses on the needs of people rather than on the accomplishments of things.

The three most effective times to think about the important relationships of our lives are during the three transitions that each day contains—early morning as we get up, late afternoon or early evening when we return from work, and late evening at bedtime. Step three is a decision to concentrate exclusively on relationships during these three transition times.

Use a highlighter or nonpenetrating marker to make

three "relationship bands" or spaces across each day—one early in the morning, one late in the evening, and one around dinnertime—reserved spaces where you will work on relationships instead of achievements. The bands reserve or set aside a little time early in the morning for meditation or planning or maybe a family prayer; a little debriefing time after work or after school when you ask questions of interest and concern, shift gears from the concerns of your job, and get your mind on the people you live with; and a little time in the evening, perhaps for tucking children in bed, or talking with your spouse, or calling a friend. The bands only take up a few minutes of the day, but if you don't put them on your days before you start scheduling, the time will get swallowed up by the less important details, errands, and "have-to-dos."

It's not necessary to write anything in the bands—or plan anything specific for them. Just reserve the time for yourself and your family, to enjoy the moments together and to tend to whatever needs come up.

A daily page, altered to include both priority blanks and relationship bands, will look something like the next page in this book.

∧ Do Aerobics
> Discuss "Boy Problem" with Lisa
∠ Get Jim's support on new idea

Try step three for ten days. You will find that the transition times, reserved by the relationship bands, become the most relaxing as well as the most rewarding parts of your day. When the habit is formed, move on to step four.

STEP 4. SERENDIPITY LINE

A top-to-bottom line placed on a daily schedule to separate the "planned things" from the spontaneous opportunities and needs that cannot be planned. *Serendipity* means the ability, through awareness and flexibility, to find something good while seeking something else; and *jumping the line* refers to the process of being aware enough and flexible enough to notice the serendipity side of life and to jump across to something spontaneous and unplanned two or three times every day.

Code the pages of your life by drawing a vertical line right down the center of each day and labeling the right-hand side "serendipity." Write your schedule on the left, leaving the right-hand side blank—as a reminder to stay aware, to stay observant, to keep the "blinders" off and notice happy surprises, unexpected opportunities, new acquaintances, unplanned needs, and anything and everything else that could not have been planned or scheduled.

Commit yourself to jumping over the "spontaneity line" at least a couple of times during the day in an effort to keep yourself awake and flexible and to keep things exciting.

A fully coded antiplanning page will look something like the next page in this book.

^ Do Aerobics
> Discuss "Boy Problem" with Lisa
< Get Jim's support on new idea

Serendipity:

Most planning starts with scheduling and with a quick listing of demands, commitments, and "have-to-dos." Things like family, personal needs, and relationships are left off or left until last. And spontaneity's killed, buried under the heaviness of "the list."

With antiplanning, the process is reversed. We start with our priority lines, relationship bands, and serendipity line, committing ourselves to them before we start listing things. Then, when we do write our schedule, it might look something like the next page in this book (depending on your own preferences and style, you may make a list as detailed as the one that follows, or you may do a much simpler list).

∧ Do Aerobics
> Discuss "Boy Problem" with Lisa
∠ Get Jim's support on new idea

	Serendipity:
6:30 Up-ready	
6:45 Aerobics, shower	
7:30 Breakfast meeting (Sharon)	
8:30 office - Bills - memos (inc. Steve) - Phone calls - call Pete for lunch	
10:30 meeting-Production	
11:30 Prepare arguments for Jim	
12:45 Lunch – Pete	
1:30 Plant inspection	
2:30 Jim-win his approval	
3:30 answer mail make sales calls	
5. Pick up Lisa after school-talk	

6:30 Home-news-mail	
7 Dinner w/Family	
call uncle Ben (how feeling?)	
9:00 Johnson reception	

Note that the three priorities got on the schedule. They always will once the three priority blanks identify them and recognize them. They seldom will if you just start scheduling and doing without thinking.

Note also that nothing is written on the "serendipity side" or in the relationship bands. Don't plan things for these spaces. Instead, train yourself to be more aware . . . of people, of situations, of need, of beauty, of opportunity. When your awareness shows you something more worthwhile than what you'd planned to do, be flexible enough (and brave enough) to jump over the line and do it.

Jot down the serendipity things and the relationship things as they happen or *after* you do them. You are writing them down not as a plan or a schedule but as a *result*—as a good memory and as a compliment to yourself for noticing them and choosing them.

By the end of your day, your page might look like the next page in this book.

meditation, reading

^ Do Aerobics

> Discuss "Boy Problem" with Lisa

∠ Get Jim's support on new idea

6:30 Up-ready
6:45 Aerobics, shower
7:30 Breakfast meeting (Sharon)
8:30 office
- Bills
- ~~memos~~
~~(inc. Steve)~~
- phone calls
- call Pete for lunch

10:30 meeting- Production
11:30 Prepare arguments for Jim
~~12:15 Lunch-Pete~~
1:30 Plant inspection
2:30 Jim-win his approval
3:30 answer mail
make sales calls
5. Pick up Lisa after school-talk

Serendipity:

Met Tom Alexander with Apex - originally from San Mateo - married - 2 kids - interested in the power project - secretary's name: Jan

Bookstore - found houseboat idea

changed strategy: Got Jim's dept. involved instead of just "winning him over"

Talked with Billy about math test

6:30 Home-news-mail

7 Dinner w/Family

call uncle Ben (how feeling?)

~~9:00 Johnson Reception~~

Patty not home yet
Beautiful evening
Lisa volunteered to start dinner. Took little Joe to zoo for an hour (Remember his face when he watched the gibbon monkeys "play tag")
Finished w/Billy on math - got into discussion of "what he wants to be"

planned tomorrow w/ Patty

The day was rather well planned, but it didn't go exactly according to plan. The person in this example wasn't troubled by this fact—on the contrary. He chose to "jump the line" several times, either because circumstances prevented him from doing what he had planned or because something came up that was more important (or more worthwhile or more beneficial) than what he had planned. He was interrupted in the morning when Bill Alexander dropped by, and he could have just said a brief hello and gone back to his memo. But he sensed an opportunity and ended up talking to Bill for over an hour.

He had planned to eat with Pete, but when Pete couldn't go, he browsed the bookstore instead and noticed a book on houseboats that gave him an idea about how his family could achieve the "ultimate vacation" they had been talking about.

When his wife Patty was late getting home, instead of being upset that they wouldn't have dinner together, he started cooking and then let Lisa (with whom he had just finished a personal talk) continue while he took his youngest boy to the park for an hour.

Later that evening, Billy had a problem with his homework that was more important than dropping by at a business reception as he had planned.

Note that when "serendipity things" have come up, they have been written in across the line, and things he decided not to do (in favor of the serendipity) have been crossed off. The crossing off doesn't mean he did them—it means he *didn't* do them . . . *chose* not to. Maybe tomorrow he will come back to some of them.

Note also that what is written on the serendipity side and in the relationship bands is in the past tense. He didn't plan to talk about Billy's worries about his math test. What he did was save that time to listen and pay attention to people he cares about. Billy brought up the math test because he was listening. After the fact, he wrote the incident in on the relationship band.

This is not to say that he didn't plan anything that has to do with relationships. Picking up Lisa and calling Uncle Ben were both things he decided to do as he thought about priorities. These things were scheduled—but not in the relationship bands. These bands are the few minutes set aside to listen and feel in the present tense—to be especially aware of the people you are with or thinking about that moment.

STEPS 1–4. FINE-TUNING THE PROCESS OF DAILY BALANCE

What is the best time for the five-minute sit-there? For some (the type of person who might be called a "lark"), the best time is first thing in the morning while the mind is fresh. For others (who might be called "owls"), the best time seems to be the late evening—looking ahead and thinking about tomorrow so they can sleep on it.

Decide for yourself whether you are a "lark" or an "owl." If you are not sure, experiment by trying it both ways.

You also need to make a decision of what type of schedule book you will carry. You will need to have a separate page for each day, and we suggest monthly booklets so that you will not be carrying something too big or too bulky. The other advantage of a monthly booklet is that you change books at the first of each month, which provides the kind of review that we suggest be a part of your Sunday Session on the first Sunday of each month. Special monthly *Lifebalance* booklets are available (see the last page of this book), or you may adapt any day-by-day schedule book simply by adding priority blanks, relationship bands, and serendipity lines.

So . . . there you have the daily process for balance. Now, the next thing we're going to tell you is that it has to be done every day, right? That you must never let a day go by without a five-minute sit-there . . . right?

Wrong. This is not some monastery you're entering—or some performance contract you are signing in blood. On the contrary, this is something you will do because you enjoy it, because it will add excitement to your life along with an extra measure of calmness and balance. Remember, it's rigid structure we're trying to get away from.

We suggest you don't fill out anything too specific on weekends. Let Saturday be a day to get away from goals . . . to do what comes naturally. You may need to make a list of household chores or errands, but keep it simple and easy. Use Sunday for rest, worship, and the kind of deeper reflection talked about in the next section.

The daily lifebalance form we have illustrated is basically for weekdays. And even on weekdays, don't demand 100 percent. If you miss a day—not holding a five-minute sit-there, not filling in the priority blanks, and so forth—don't worry about it. You'll still have the weekly balance form, which will be discussed next, and it may actually be good to miss a day once in a while as a change of pace.

Try to be consistent in daybalancing for the first three or four weeks, however. By then you will be in the habit and fully aware of the quality the process can add to your life. From then on you will use daybalance not because you have to but because you want to.

Daybalancing, and the effective use of priority blanks, relationship bands, and the serendipity line, can change the way you feel, the way you think, and the way you live.

As you learn the art of working the triangle, jumping the line, and reserving time through relationship bands, you will develop a balance that will minimize stress and frustration even as it helps you accomplish more that is meaningful.

One of the first things you will notice and appreciate is that your definition of a perfect day will change.

If before lifebalance you were a structured person who made long lists and got your jollies by crossing things off your list as you did them (and when you did something not on your list, you quickly wrote it on so you could cross it off) . . . if you were that kind of person, your definition of a perfect day will change from:

> "a day when I cross everything off"
>
> to
>
> "a day when I cross off the most important things but also have some spontaneous, unplanned happy accidents."

And if, before lifebalance, you were an unstructured person who would usually "go with the flow" and do whatever came up or seemed most pressing at the moment . . . if you were that kind of person, your definition of a perfect day will change from:

> "a day when everything just seemed to go well"
>
> to

"a day when I decided what was most important in the three areas of my life and *chose* to do them; and still had time for flexibility."

After you have changed your definitions and formed the habits of daybalancing, go on to step five.

STEP 5. SUNDAY SAW SHARPENING

(Sunday Sessions for weekbalancing): Taking a few minutes the first day of the week to decide what is most important during the seven days ahead.

Our mental saws need weekly sharpening!

The daily five-minute sit-there just discussed is definitely the key to daybalance, but it can't really qualify as saw sharpening. Genuine sharpening requires a longer period of deeper thought—at least a half hour a week. And the best time to do it is on the first day—on Sunday. Deciding in advance what you will try to do during the week ahead for each balance point will make daily balancing easier and more natural.

Set aside a half hour (or more if you prefer) each Sunday to think about the week ahead. Once again, use the triangle model and think about your work, about your family, and about yourself, both in terms of what you need and in terms of what service you can give to others. Lay out or draw your week on a full sheet of paper.

As with daybalancing, avoid thinking first about what you have to do during the coming week. Think first about what you *want* to do and *choose* to do in each of the three priorities or balance points of life, *then* (after thinking about the priority areas) begin to think about what you will do when and to consider each day of the coming week.

The Sunday Session example on the opposite page will help you to understand the concept of saw sharpening. Despite (or perhaps because of) its simplicity, this format can be of great assistance in balancing and prioritizing a week. The specific examples included may or may not fit your own situation or needs—but it will give you the idea.

The three balance points (work, family, and self) are represented by the three boxes at the top of the page. The work box appears on the left not because it is first, but because it is usually a left brain, achievement-oriented function. (See lifebalance symbol and discussion on page 226.) The self balance point is in the middle because a balanced self requires equal emphasis on right brain relationships and left brain accomplishments. The family balance point is on the right because of the flexibility and right brain insight that families require.

Setting up and using this type of form is simple. Write down, inside the three squares, the most important things you can do for each priority or balance point during the coming week. Put an open circle by each thing you list (which you can color in to signify completion).

Once again, it is important to do this *first,* before you begin to think about the schedule or requirements of the week ahead. The great failure or error of most typical weekly planning is that it begins with the listing of obligations and with filling up the time without any effort to consider what is most important. Then, typically, we finish that process and say to ourselves, "Busy week again—darn it—no time for family or personal needs."

Weekbalance and the Sunday Session *reverse* this pro-

<

- Finish 1/3 of month's sales quota
- Improve relationship with Bart in shipping dept.
- move bank account – get interest on checking
- Get car inspected
- Pay first of month bills

^

- Run 15 miles
- Read Scripture (15 chapters)
- "Day balance" everyday (work the triangle)
- Finish cancer drive assignment
- 1 hour of volunteer work at hospital

>

- Family outing (dinner and movie – celebrate first anniversary in house)
- Flowers or poetry to Patty
- Get in touch with Aunt Jane (help with her move?)
- Help Tim on 7-8-9 timetables
- Eat together at least 3 nights
- Write letter to Lance in Switzerland

SUNDAY	MONDAY	TUESDAY	WEDNESDAY	THURSDAY	FRIDAY	SATURDAY
Read Scripture	Run 5 mi		Run 5 mi	call Aunt Jane (before 7:00)	Run 5 mi	~~Sping~~ Spring cleaning (yard)
Church	WORK					
"Sunday Sessions"	visit with Bart when I bring orders down	Change bank account	Final appointments to finish quote	12:00 car inspected	order flowers	
Family meeting (plan week together)	Family outing	Eat ~~together~~	Basketball Tickets	Eat together	S. to piano lesson	Fishing with boys
		Pay bills		Cancer Drive	symphony	
Day balance	"	"	"	"	"	"
	scriptures		scriptures		scriptures	

cess. You think first about the most important areas of life, and decide or choose what to do about each during the week ahead.

Then you use the little calendar below to jot down when you will do those priorities and to fit them in with the other obligations and schedules of the week ahead. Don't fill the calendar with details. You can save that for daybalance. Just use the calendar to decide when you will tend to your priorities and to block out a graphic overview of the week ahead.

You will find, when you take a full half hour in a Sunday Session to think about your coming week, that your mind will identify for you what is important in each area. You will then find that, with your weekbalance complete, daybalancing during the week ahead will become both easier and more rewarding.

Hold Sunday Sessions for two or three consecutive weeks. You will find an improvement in the quality of how you are spending your time, and your daily balancing flows from your Sunday plan (and adds up to its completion by the end of the week). When you feel comfortable with Sunday Sessions, go on to step six.

STEP 6. "FIRST SUNDAY" SUNDAY SESSION

An expanded Sunday Session, held on the first Sunday of the month, in which one evaluates the month just past and creates in the mind a balanced view of the month ahead.

Just as daybalancing is aided by weekly goals, weekbalancing is assisted and made more effective by monthly goals and priorities.

The best time to think about the month ahead is in an expanded Sunday Session on the first Sunday of each month or the last Sunday of the previous month.

The process is very similar to weekbalancing. Discipline yourself to think first about what you ought to do and choose to do during the month ahead in each of the three priority areas. Then fit these things in with the events and schedules for the month in the weekday and weekend spaces that take up the bottom of the page.

The example on the following page will help you design a simple form for your own monthbalancing. Notice that each week consists of a block for the five weekdays and a second, smaller block for the weekend. Note also that there is no effort to do any detailed planning—only to list the main activities and focus points for each week and to decide when the goals for each balance point (above) will be done.

STEP 7. RIGHT BRAIN RETENTION

Keeping track of the ideas and insights that come spontaneously or in "flashes" as well as the unexpected people, needs, and opportunities that cross one's life.

As you practice lifebalancing on a daily basis, you will accumulate, on the pages of your daily schedules, numerous notes about ideas, people, and events that you want to retain and that you may wish to refer back to.

There will be times when you want to refer back to the left side schedule . . . to recall when you did something or to review your activities for a specific day. More

o Reach sales quota o Invest 1/10 of month's income o Look into possibility of trading car—make decision o Proposal written for combining sales areas o Get smoother cooperation with shipping dept.	o In training for 10 K race (37:00) o Read two books from New Testament o Resume volunteer work o Be up at 6 each day—have personal time before breakfast	o Get new back lawn put in back o Improve order and neatness in the home o Individual "Daddy date" with each child

Observe shipping order dept. Start draft of proposal Family meeting on ORDER Lisa's Daddy date	New grass—spring cleaning (yard + house) Sunday Scripture study	Run 15 mi
M-T-W (Detroit trip) First half of sales quota final Billy's Daddy date	Weekend family trip Church	Run 15 mi
Locate investment options Decision on car Tim's Daddy date	Volunteer work in Hospital Church	Run 15 mi
Finish sales quota, finish proposal Thurs-Fri (sales convention in DePaul)	Overnight camping Church	Run 15 mi

often, however, you will wish to refer to something on the right side of a particular day. And it will usually be an idea, a spontaneous event, or notes you made about a new person you met.

It gets harder and harder to find these notes as time passes . . . unless you keep a simple chronological index of the things you want to remember.

Usually when you want to recall something, you have a pretty close idea of when it happened, so you can find it by checking your index for the period of time during which you think it occurred.

If you set up your index like the following example, then your date column will tell you when it happened, and how far across the page you make your entry will tell you whether it referred to an idea, an event, or a person.

Date	Event:	Idea:	Person:
5-16	Incredible sunset—see poem		Tom Alexander—from San mateo—3 Kids—Sec: Jan
5-17		Try backing up the Reinforcement with the new adhesive from Syms	
5-19	Went to concert on Impulse—moved by final concerto!		Took Billy to meet ballplayers at Park
5-20		Take whole family to new Caravelle campground some weekend	Anne Russell—Billy's math teacher—said we would call
5-22	Remarkable article in *Time* (see notes)	might want to look into Billows Co. as possible publisher for next training manual	

At the end of a month (in your monthly "First Sunday" Sunday Session), take the time to go back through the previous month's daily balance sheets and notes (or the daily pages in whatever kind of scheduling book you are using). When you come to notes on any event, idea, or person that you want to retain and have access to, enter it (with as few words as possible) on the right day and in the correct column of your idea index.

You will enjoy the right brain retention process. It will refresh your memory and put things where you can find them. . . . And it will allow you to relive the best moments of the month just passed.

Try the *"First Sunday" Sunday Session*, complete with *right brain retention*, for a couple of months. When you feel comfortable with them, go on to step eight.

STEPS 1–7. A SMALL INVESTMENT OF TIME

Just in case (at first reading) steps one through seven look time-consuming, please accept our promise that they are actually *time-saving.* Out of the 168 hours in a week, the *Lifebalance* system requires only one hour (five minutes per day for the "sit-there," and thirty minutes for the Sunday Session). That one hour can dramatically increase the quality as well as the effectiveness of the other 167.

STEP 8. LONG-RANGE "L GOALS"

Things one wants to achieve during the next year (or longer). These goals usually involve lists, logic, and the left brain, so we call them L goals. The *yearly day away* is the day (ideally in a retreat setting) that is devoted to sorting out these balanced long-range L goals.

Forming the habit of establishing a single priority each day for family, work, and self, using relationship bands, and developing the awareness that prompts regular jumping the line into serendipity will greatly increase a person's lifebalance.

And spending a few saw sharpening moments every Sunday to set weekly and monthly goals as a target for the daily priorities to aim at will further enhance that balance.

Still, many people will want to go further. They will want to know that their balancing is adding up to something longer-range. They may worry that what they are planning each day and each week and each month is too often based on what is expected or required of them at the moment—rather than on what they choose or believe or want for themselves and for their lives.

Lifebalance reaches its purest form and produces its finest results (and its greatest joy) when daily and weekly prioritizing is "backed up" by balanced longer-range goals.

It is extremely hard mental work to establish yearly and longer-range goals. Once they are set, however, Sunday Sessions become far more effective, and daily and weekly balancing becomes part of a grand design.

Step eight involves getting away for at least one full, uninterrupted day each year to project all three balance points into the future. Spend this yearly getaway in a place that is conducive to thought and meditation. Being away from home, office, and normal surroundings will sharpen your perspective.

Think with pencil in hand. Make notes, draw diagrams, doodle, dream a little. Deal with all three balance points. Arrange your goals around the three corners of the lifebalance triangle. What do you want to accomplish over the next several years (and particularly during the coming years) in your work or career? What do you want to bring to pass in your personal life, within your own body and your own character? And what do you want to see happen in your family? How do your goals in each of the three areas relate to each other? What are the things you can do during the coming year that will really matter ten, or fifteen, or even twenty years from now?

Before your day away ends, try to simplify. Boil your thoughts down to a few clear goals for each balance point. Then look at the months of the year and make some decisions about when you will do what.

This type of thinking and projecting is fun and imaginative, but it is also difficult and mentally taxing. You may come home with a headache. But what an investment this day away can be. Once you have thought through the year ahead, you will have a course to follow, a track to run on, and a foundation and framework for daily and weekly balancing all through the coming year.

STEP 9. LONG-RANGE "R GOALS"

Goals that deal with people rather than things. These goals involve relationships and the intuitive right hemisphere of the brain, so they are called R goals. When we set R goals to go with our L goals, we have created *two-edged goals*.

It is important to note that R goals are very different from L goals (just as relationships are different and require different things than achievements). But it is also important to realize that, despite their difference, L goals and R goals are very similar in terms of how they work. In both cases we have to be specific enough about our goals that we can literally see them as accomplished in our minds. Thus, with an L goal, we write it down or list it and work until we can cross it off our list. With an R goal, we write it down by describing a relationship the way we want it to be. In either case, what we have written is a mental conception of something that we then go out and (consciously and subconsciously) pursue and achieve.

R goals are produced not through the logical or sequential analysis, but through the kind of visualizing and imagining that you can do with your right brain.

The only way to get R goals on paper is through description. Use part of your yearly day away to attempt to visualize as clearly as you possibly can the type of person you want to be in one year's time—and the kind of relationships you want to have by then. Then you describe your future self and your future relationships.

Begin with pen and paper by trying to describe the relationship you want to have with yourself at the end of your year.

Then describe your future relationship with your spouse. Then with your children, then with your best friends. Don't worry too much about being realistic. After all, you are not describing what exists now; you are describing what you want to exist in the future, at the end of this year you are thinking through.

Remember the principle involved here. If you can

clearly imagine and describe a much improved relationship—if you can or envision it in your mind—then you can obtain it. Your subconscious mind and the whole intuitive, magical right hemisphere of your brain will point you and propel you toward the actions and attitudes that will turn your description from a wish or a dream into reality.

A relationship description of "self" might start something like this:

> I have just turned thirty-eight years old and am feeling more secure about myself and more happy with my life than ever before. I take excellent care of myself. Physically I am in much better shape than I was a year ago. I'm more observant and sensitive, and I seem to get more enjoyment from everyday life. . . .
>
> I am honest with myself and I can admit that . . . etc.

A relationship description for a spouse might begin something like this:

> Patty is now thirty-six. We have been married now for fifteen years and are more in love than ever. We share every feeling and have thrown out the idea that some things are better left unsaid. We are true partners in that we plan together. We respect and admire each other and appreciate our differences. We're learning to be patient and gentle with each other and to prioritize each other

above everything else, even the children. We find that we can . . . etc.

Sometimes it is easiest to describe a desired relationship by actually picking an event in the future, or a particular place and thing—and then describing a relationship on that day and in that place. For example, a relationship description with a son might start like this:

> Tommy is now nine years old. It is the opening day of fishing season and we are alone together in the early morning, fishing on the sandy bank of the Logan River. There is a real joy in being together. He knows how proud I am of him and I feel his pride in me. No subject is off-limits. He asks me about friends, about a problem in school, even about the facts of life. I'm always honest with him, and I always have time to listen. After he catches his first fish of the morning, he looks at me and says . . . etc.

When you get your R goal descriptions the way you want them, put them with your L goals and you will have the kind of two-edged goals that will serve as a framework for the balancing you will do in your weekly Sunday Sessions during the coming year.

EPILOGUE

Tightrope walkers stroll along a high wire with the ease that most of us walk down the street. They do so with the aid of a balance bar—the long pole they carry that stabilizes and steadies their progress.

To stay steady and balanced on the tightrope of life, we need our own kind of balance bar—one made up of strong commitments to clear priorities and of thought patterns that focus both our plans and our sensitivity on the things that really matter.

Anwar Sadat's once stated: "He who cannot change the very fabric of his thought, will never be able to change reality."

No one changes the fabric of a person's thought but that person. Your balance bar, in other words, will have to be of your own making. But you may have found some of the building materials in this volume.

Richard:

It had been a couple of months since we had finished the manuscript for this book. We had set it on the shelf to simmer for a time so we could read through and edit it with a fresh perspective.

When we read it again, something became very clear to us: *Balance is a formula for joy.*

There is more satisfaction and pleasure in work and in the process of accomplishing things in the outside world. But the deeper joys spring from what happens inside our homes and inside ourselves.

We've avoided the use of the word "success" throughout the book, so let us use the word twice in the last sentence. *Lifebalance means balancing the outer success of work and career with the inner success of family and personal growth.*

While this is the end of a book, we hope that it is, for you, the beginning of a process—and perhaps the beginning of a quest for more quality and more balance in life.

Balance, like most other truly worthwhile things, is something we never completely attain, but something we can always be obtaining. The tightrope walker is never balanced in the sense of being still or stationary—he is always balancing, and gradually becoming better at his balancing.

In reality, balancing is a skill that can become an art—an art we can master only when it is our conscious goal.

OVERVIEW

ACKNOWLEDGMENTS TO:

1. Friends and brothers like the Downeys, the Archibalds, the Mackeys, the Stewarts, the Mayfields, the Chris Eyres, and the Petersens, who read the manuscript long before it was balanced.

2. Corry DeMille, who retyped it so often that it threatened her own balance.

3. Our nine children, who are our prime motivators and reason for wanting to be balanced.

ABOUT THE AUTHORS

Richard and Linda Eyre were living the book *Lifebalance* long before they wrote it. Richard is a Harvard M.B.A. who runs several businesses, has twenty books in print, writes poetry, enters tennis and windsurfing tournaments, and has had several presidential appointments in Washington. Linda is a concert violinist, writer, teacher, and was named by the National Council of Women as one of America's six outstanding young women.

The Eyres' highest priority is their family, which consists of nine natural children plus a student from Mainland China (not to mention the dogs, cats, gerbils, and other residents). They have homes in Salt Lake City, Jackson Hole, Wyoming, and Washington, D.C.

They don't believe anyone should pattern their life after theirs, but they do believe there is enough time to do a great many things and that everyone can find that time through their own form of lifebalance.

NOW AVAILABLE

1. *Lifebalance "anti-planners"*

Set of twelve monthly "anti-planner" booklets with each daily page incorporating "priority blanks," "spontaneity lines," and "relationship bands."

2. *Lifebalance Seminars*

A ten-part, in-home *Lifebalance* Seminar (each part consisting of an audio-tape and printed supplements, forms, and worksheets).

3. *Lifebalance Newsletter*

Ten issues per year, each containing new ideas and concepts of *Lifebalance.*